Apartheid

UNA D. BRUHNS

 FriesenPress

One Printers Way
Altona, MB R0G 0B0
Canada

www.friesenpress.com

Edited by Bernice Lever
Foreword by Carla Schafer

Note to reader:
This book is a memoir. It depicts actual events in the authors' life truthfully as recollections of experiences over time and veritable by research, some events abridged. All persons are genuine individuals; I have changed the names of some individuals to respect their privacy.

ISBN
978-1-03-914777-5 (Hardcover)
978-1-03-914776-8 (Paperback)
978-1-03-914778-2 (eBook)

1. Biography & Autobiography, Personal Memoirs

Distributed to the trade by The Ingram Book Company

PREFACE

I've written this book for my son, nieces, nephews,

and all oppressed generations to come.

Don't let someone else define who you are.

Dedicated to battered women, men and sexual assault victims.

Break the cycle: speak up and get out while you can.

DEDICATION

To my son, Lance.

In gratitude, I thank my husband, Juergen, for giving us a new start in life. For his patience in assisting and encouraging me in all my endeavours.

I thank my parents for sacrificing their dignity in an unfair society to improve our lives.

ACKNOWLEDGEMENTS:

I want to express my gratitude to the following people:

- Carla Shafer and Bernice Lever for giving me a kickstart.
- Ruth Kozak for her encouragement.
- Wren-Writers New Westminster, for their constructive critiques:
- David Burnell
- John Taylor
- Donna Terrill
- David Hutchinson
- Val Mossop
- Tiberia Pacheco
- Helga Parekh

Una Bruhns is a published poet.

An Award-winning writer, she received a Haiku Sakura Award at the Cherry Blossom Festival in 2008, the Community Ambassadors Award from the Writers International Network in 2015 and the Tanka Award from the North Shore Writers Association in 2016.

She resides in New Westminster, British Columbia with her spouse.

My story is cast in Johannesburg, South Africa, during Apartheid. I was not content to be oppressed by the regime, where there was no room for growth. I never felt like I belonged and was lost in a crowd, withering in the African sun.

Longing to be free, I uprooted myself from where I was born. With God's guidance and my parents' blessings, I knew I'd survive wherever I went. I have no regrets about the path that I took.

Chapter One

In 1939, my mother, who we lovingly referred to as Mumsie, gave birth to me six months before World War II in Vrededorp, "*Village of Peace* in Johannesburg, South Africa, established by Paul Kruger in 1893," was one of the oldest communities and the first multicultural suburb, located between Braamfontein and Brixton cemeteries and close to the city centre. It extended from 1st Street, ending on 25th Street, edged by Krause Street in the west and Solomon Street in the east.[1]

I was the third child of five siblings: Maureen, Veronica, me (Una, nicknamed Sally), Neville, and Patsy.

When I was six years old, Mumsie's sister, Helen, suddenly died, leaving her two children, Pearl and Desmond. Mumsie adopted Pearl, and we became six. Another family member assumed the responsibility for her brother, Desmond.

We were a modest bunch of kids, surviving through a rough, simple, noisy, crowded time with no superficial wrappings. Our home was our place of refuge, where Mumsie ruled and obedience was paramount.

I vividly recall our three-roomed, semi-detached home on 18th Street, at the end of a cluster of four with a lane leading to the backyard. We were cordoned off from the following four groups by a seven-foot corrugated metal fence.

1   https://www.sahistory.org.za/place/pageview

We shared an outside faucet with cold running water, a clothesline, and a toilet. The toilet resembled an enamelled bedpan embedded into the cement floor with two bricks on either side that enabled us to sit in a squatting position. *The Rand Daily Mail Newspaper* was our substitute for toilet paper.

We always entered the house through the backdoor. My parents reserved the front entrance for guests. Our kitchen measured eight by ten feet. The floor was made of sand that we kept compacted by sprinkling it with a combination of water and DDT, a disinfectant.

In the corner, opposite the yellow-checkered curtained one-pane kitchen window, stood a two-plated coal stove. Two homemade shelves, strong enough to hold pots and pans, adjoined the furnace, one above the other. The bottom shelf held neatly piled dinner plates. The underside had screwed-in hooks to hang enamelled mugs that children could reach.

We enjoyed all our meals at our long wooden kitchen table.

It was standard for us to take turns bathing in the old, galvanized bath filled with hot water from the pot on the coal stove, adding Dettol to the bathwater.

Adjacent to the kitchen was my parents' bedroom with its bare wooden floor. Sparsely furnished with a double bed, the mattress was stuffed with coir matting material manufactured from the husks of coconuts. The shams on the bed were lace-edged and stiffly starched. Next to the bed stood a round table covered with a dusty rose linen tablecloth, where sat a porcelain washbasin and jug.

When I was older, we took turns scrubbing the bedroom floor. Wood splinters penetrated the palms of our hands or embedded under our fingernails, where we could see the splint through the top of our nails. We had to wait until the nail grew to remove it; sometimes, it got infected.

Adjoining their bedroom was the front room, which was the entrance to the house. This room contained a sideboard that served as a pantry. We also sat out a couple of padded chairs for visitors.

At night, we would roll our coir mattresses out in the entrance where my sisters, brother, and I slept after we were scrubbed clean, slathered with Vaseline, and said prayers. We would then blow out the flame of the kerosene lamp and darkness would descend.

My parents left for work at 6 a.m. each workday. My father worked at a steel manufacturing company, and my mother in the garment industry.

My grandfather, my mother's father, and two uncles, Oscar and Leon, lived next door.

As soon as my parents left for work, my grandfather would enter through the front door.

"Get up," he shouted. Then, ripping the blankets off our warm bodies, he took the bed covers with him to assure himself that we would stay up and get ready for school.

My two elder sisters, Maureen and Veronica, prepared breakfast, comprising of cornmeal porridge or Maltabella porridge, a brown malted Sorghum that was always lumpy.

Pearl and I spit out most lumps and threw them into the garbage can. We also had hot mugs of milo, a chocolate-flavoured malted powder mixed with hot water, and each a slice of brown bread slathered with peanut butter.

Lunch was provided at our school, including milk, sweet buns, and a piece of fruit. We had black bean soup served from a large bucket and ladled into our enamelled mugs during the winter months. I always lingered at the back of the lineup. I would check how low the soup was in the bucket, allowing a few students to move ahead because I knew most of the beans were in the bottom and the consistency would be thicker. It filled my belly until I got home.

Muslim Neighbours

An obese woman, Mrs. Kumar, and her family occupied the first house in the cluster of four. Her obesity prevented her from walking. Instead, she sat in her kitchen, looking through the window, observing the backyard's "ins and outs." When her daughter, Asa, had a baby, there were no throw-away diapers during this time. Instead, towelled napkins were the custom. These napkins had to be washed daily and hung out to dry. Mrs. Kumar kept an eye on the clothesline and the sky, and as soon as she noticed any threatening clouds, she bellowed, "Asa, the black clouds are coming; bring in the piss blankets."

Our neighbours, the Samodien family and the Kumar family, were Muslim. During their holy month of Ramadan, they fast from dawn to dusk. So, when the Muslim wives prepared their meals for the immediate eight-hour cessation, the aromas of curries and jasmine rice and the baking of sweet pastries permeated the air.

As is their custom, they prepared extra food to share with their neighbours during this time. We always looked forward to their cuisine's spicy flavours during Ramadan. Sometimes, I would visit Mrs. Samodien to watch her prepare special meals for her family. If I liked a particular dish, I made mental notes. Muslims are not allowed to eat any food cooked in a Christian home. In the Muslim religion, they believe gammon is unclean.

Solley, an alcoholic, lived on the other side of the corrugated fence. He owned a Vervet monkey with a silver-grey body, a marked black face, and white-ridged eyebrows, feet, and tail. Its genitals were vividly coloured, namely a red penis and a blue scrotum that my grandfather referred to as the "blue ass monkey."

Solley tied the monkey to a long metal chain to run along the metal fence, showing its long canine teeth. When Solley was inebriated, he unchained the monkey, allowing it to terrorize the neighbourhood, attacking the dogs and cats. Terrified, we all stayed indoors until the monkey was tied -up.

When I was about five or six years old, locusts invaded South Africa, blacking the skies. They flew in by the millions, making an eerie humming sound as they scoured the countryside, eating all the farmer's crops. They stuck to our windowpanes with their spindly legs, peering at us with bulging eyes. It reminded me of the plagues from the bible stories.

Mumsie baked scrumptious coconut tarts. She always bought two dozen eggs for baking packed in brown paper bags, filled with sawdust to prevent cracking. She also bought coconut flakes packed in brown bags. All dried goods were in the cupboard in the front room. My sister Pearl and I loved coconut flakes.

While Mumsie was bathing my sister Patsy in the kitchen, we snuck into the front room to help ourselves to some coconut. First, we would blindly feel the packets without looking into them.

Then, nervously watching for Mumsie, we stuck our hands into the packages for a healthy handful of flakes and quickly shoved it into our mouths, only to discover it was sawdust from the packaged eggs. Just then, Mumsie walked into the room and caught us with our mouths filled with sawdust, gagging, coughing, and trying to breathe. We must have looked ridiculous!

Mumsie kept her composure, chuckling. "Clean up the mess, rinse out your mouths. And for being disobedient, you won't get any tarts." After cleaning up, we stayed out of sight by reading in the bedroom.

Vignette

Saturday 7 a.m. laundry day.

Our eyes filled with sleep

We placed the galvanized bathtub

On the slightly elevated drain in the backyard.

Helped my father carry out buckets of hot water to fill the tub.

We hated the rough scrubbing, rubbing, and slapping of the garments.

Some were stained with red earth.

The cold early morning air made our eyes and noses burn.

Slap, slap, rinse, then hanged to dry.

The bathtub emptied for the next load.

Steaming bedsheets reeked of caustic soda.

Wooden cloth pegs held laundry on the clothesline.

I longed to muse as sunlight streamed through the slits of our back-yard fencing.

We were the son and daughters of the deacon scrub, slap, rinse, hands bled.

"Breakfast call." The wind blew wet laundry billowing on the clothesline.

I look back at what shaped us then and still does.

School Rules

Most of the children in the neighbourhood attended Krause Street School, which was within walking distance of our homes. We were a multicultural group of children without bias.

Every morning, before classes commenced, the entire school would assemble to recite the Lord's Prayer. School uniforms were compulsory.

Girls wore white shirts and black gyms: pleated uniform dresses with pleats, and a black sash tied at the waist. Our hair had to be plaited and tied with red ribbons. Boys wore short pants, white shirts, and neckties.

We could not afford satin ribbons, so my uncle Oscar took us to an area in the cemetery where the graveyard cleaners discarded all the decaying wreaths. We removed the best ribbons from the wires on the wreaths.

"You better work fast, or those dead people will come after you," Oscar said as he hurried us on.

The stench from the decaying flowers burned our nostrils. We quickly searched for the best ribbons. Finally, we washed out the wire's rust marks and ironed and folded them, ready for use.

Oscar, Mumsie's younger brother, volunteered his services in the army. After the war, he returned home a damaged man, suffering from shellshock, now coined as a post-traumatic stress disorder. There was no medical or professional counselling available. He tried to commit suicide by swallowing caustic soda, which liquefied in his mouth, causing his jaw to lock while the bubbling caustic soda ate away the inside of his cheeks and tongue.

Both sides of his face were cut, and pipes were inserted into his mouth to remove the sodium, leaving him with scars resembling a smile. He would joke about his scars and scare us when we were little by pretending to be the boogeyman.

As children, we were not allowed to wander down to the end of 18th Street because a busy main road and a rail crossing ran directly through it. The only time we were allowed further afar was when we accompanied Mumsie to 14th Street, with its small, dark stores owned by either Jewish or Indian merchants selling clothing or soft goods in stiff competition. Mumsie would choose our Christmas dresses from the Jewish merchant on a layaway plan. There were display stands with their bargain bins overflowing. Patsy would hide in those bins while we franticly searched for her.

1947 – The Royal Visit

I celebrated my eighth birthday at the end of March. At the beginning of April 1947, the principal made a special announcement: the royal family, King George VI of England, the Queen, and their daughters, Princess Elizabeth and Princess Margaret would be visiting Johannesburg on April 5. The procession was to pass our school along the main road. Each student received a Union Jack flag. Everything was abuzz with excitement.

Finally, the long-anticipated day arrived. We all looked like shiny new pennies in our school uniforms. Our class was fortunate to stand in the front row. Thousands lined the street.; People sat in trees, trying to get a better glimpse of the royals. As the procession neared, you could hear a pin drop, except for the horse's hooves.

The moment was here. As the carriage drew closer, I saw the king in his regal outfit looking very solemn. The queen's diamond-studded crown flashed in the sunlight. As they waved and smiled, cheers rang out: "God save the King."

The second carriage, with Princess Elizabeth and Princess Margaret, followed. I was so giddy with excitement.

After the procession ended, the teachers marched us back to school for refreshments. As we neared the gate, I saw Mr. Pailin, a member of our church. As soon as the teacher passed through the gate, Mr. Pailin took my hand and said, "Let's go for a walk."

I asked, "Where are we going?"

He replied, "To see the end of the parade." I hesitated, but the thought of seeing the end of the parade was exciting.

Molestation

After a long walk, we entered an old, musty, abandoned goldmine. We were surrounded by vast heaps of yellow soil with sparse tufts of grass. Mr. Pailin was a tall man with the physique of a boxer. I looked at him in fear, knowing that the king's beautiful carriage would not be coming our way. There was no parade!

I heard traffic in the distance. On that godforsaken damp clay ground, I lost my innocence forever as he molested me. He then gave me a grave warning to remain silent. He walked me back to the school gate. As I cried, he shook his finger at me and said, "Now go home and stop sniffling, and don't tell anybody what happened, do you understand? Now go on home."

Afraid to speak, I nodded my head, indicating that I understood. I walked home with tears streaming down my cheeks, feeling sick to my stomach, and trying to understand what had just transpired. In fear of being questioned about why I was so late returning home, I went straight to the toilet in the backyard, which had a faucet, and I kept splashing myself with cold water, trying to wash away the violation.

My parents were not home, yet I crawled into bed. When Mumsie arrived home, she asked, "Why are you in bed?"

I said, "I have a terrible headache."

"It must be from all the excitement of the day." Then she handed me an aspirin and a hot cup of milk and told me to rest.

I never breathed a word to anyone.

I was relieved when Mr. Pailin and his family did not attend service for the following two weeks. Then, one Sunday at church, it was announced that his family had relocated to Cape Town. I was happy that I would not see his ugly face again.

The Parade

Today is the last day I cried.
For my innocence, you took.
At eight years old,
Under the pretense,
It was a parade.

I will not give you the satisfaction.
By describing the repulsive and
Vile things you did.
The pain you caused me when
You left me alone at the gate.

The feelings that numbed me inside.
All I wanted to do was cry.
Full of fear, not wanting to tell.
Because the Bible said
I will burn in hell.

I'm glad you left without a trace.
You spared me the agony.
I never want to see your ugly face again.
Your actions made me feel unclean.

In my teenage years, I spun out of control.
You may have taken my innocence.
But I never allowed you.
To take my spirit.

I only think of you now
As a dirty scrap of paper from my past,
Blowing in the distance.
Yes, today is the last day I cried.

Chapter Two

Rebellion

I felt helpless, afraid of divulging my secret. Finally, I refrained from getting too close to my siblings and befriended Lilian, a feisty girl I admired for standing her ground against the bullies at school. Lilian taught me to scale fences, climb trees, and cuss with attitude.

One day after school, we decided to scale the fence belonging to a man we heard had turkeys on his property. We thought it would be exciting to tease them. After scouting around, we found six turkeys behind a gated area and poked at them with a stick; then, we opened the gate to see what reaction we would get. Instead, they ran out, with their gobbling faces turning hues of blue and red as they took chase after us.

This sight scared us, and we ran as fast as possible, with the turkeys at our heels. Adrenaline pumping, we cleared the fence and landed in the shallow ditch just before the owner came out to see what all the noise was. We laid low, hoping he would not see us. As soon as he got all the turkeys back behind the gate, we took off and headed home in different directions.

Two weeks later, we attended a Chinese funeral, where it was the custom to hand out tickies: a small silver three-penny piece (2 ½ cents) wrapped in red tissue paper handed to each attendee as they passed the coffin. This handout afforded us to buy a bar of sticky toffee.

Another time, we curiously wandered into a Muslim school where, for the following two weeks, we learned to read and recite the alphabet in Arabic. Fatima, whom we met at school, invited us to her home for lunch. As we entered their home, we greeted her mother in Arabic, "Salam," meaning peace/good day.

She smiled and said, "Wash your hands, and join the family." Her family was seated crossed-legged on cushions arranged in a circle on the floor, and we found a spot and sat down uncomfortably, trying to sit crossed-legged so we could fit in. Her mother dished various spicy food onto a large platter, including flatbread (*chapati*). We watched as everybody broke off pieces of bread, then delved in by scooping up the food as they ate. Lilian and I quickly exchanged glances, then immediately copied their custom, scooping up delicious mutton curry and various spicy foods. After washing our hands, we thanked Fatima's mother for the delightful meal and Fatima for the invitation, then hurried home.

At our dinner table, I said, "Mumsie, make chapatis. Dish the food into one big plate; we can scoop up the food with the chapatis. Then, there won't be that many dishes to wash."

Mumsie looked at me, raised her eyebrows, and asked, "Where were you after school today?"

Everybody at the dinner table awaited my reply. After I excitedly relayed my adventure, Mumsie replied, "I want you to stay away from Lilian."

A couple of weeks later, Lilian invited me to her home. Her brothers were going to take photos of the neighbourhood children and needed some help. So, despite Mumsie's advice, I went home with Lilian. The layout of their home differed from ours; theirs was a single-family detached home with a back gate leading out into a lane.

When we arrived, her brothers had everything set up in the backyard with a chair covered with a long, black cloth trailing to the ground.

I asked, "How can I help?"

Lilian responded, "Let the children in through the front gate one at a time."

Three children stood in line at the gate. I led the first little girl in for her photo. One of Lilian's brothers stood in front with a camera attached to a tripod. The other brother stood behind the chair.

Her one brother near the camera said, "Stand in front of the chair. Look at the camera, smile, now sit down."

Before she sat down, her other brother pulled the chair away, and the girl fell into a bath of water hidden under the chair. I was shocked as she fell into the water with a splash! Then Lilian and her brothers howled with laughter.

Lilian helped her leave via the back gate without apologizing. Her little dress was dripping wet, and she was crying. Bewildered, I ran to the front gate where the other two children were waiting and shouted, "Don't go into the yard; go home!"

The girl who fell into the tub came toward us, sobbing. I grabbed her hand, and we ran from the house. I avoided Lilian like the plague after the photoshoot.

In later years, I wondered what happened to Lilian and her brothers.

Illegal Gambling

Charlie, a Chinese man, owned the corner grocery store on 18th Street. He also ran a gambling game called Fah-fee. Each bet cost twenty-five cents.

Fah-fee used numbers to represent animals, humans, or objects in the galaxy and the ocean. For example, Bad Woman, #4; Monkey, #8; Fish, #10; Little Girl, #7; etc. The game took place twice daily. First, a young man called a runner would call on homes and collect the betting numbers and money. All the wagers were placed in a hat and drawn randomly.

Once Charlie retrieved the winning number, the runner would emerge from the store and face the road, where everyone could see him. If the monkey were the winner, he would act like a monkey or mimic a swimming fish, so everybody knew the winning number. He would then pay out the winners.

Newtown Market

Each month, on a Saturday at 5:30 a.m., all six of us children would board the bus with my father to visit the market in Newtown. The hustling, bustling, and enormity of the market amazed us. Men shouting, trying to auction off their wares of the day. Others wheeled around produce from stall to stall.

We heard thunderous laughter from a portly Italian man wearing a stained apron standing behind the fish counter. There were different sizes of fish. Huge pork, beef, and mutton carcasses hung from steel hooks. We inhaled the fragrance of rows and rows of flowers in various colours. We marvelled at vegetables we had never seen before.

Most of all, we looked forward to sampling the delicious ice cream and pastries. We took mental notes as my dad bargained for the best price on his purchases. As a result, we lugged home a bag of potatoes, oranges, and a box of green grapes. On our way back, smelling the sweetness of the grapes made us drool.

Occasionally, my parents and Maureen and Veronica went into town to shop while my grandfather tended us at his house next door. To keep us busy, he hauled out a dozen large tin cans from a cupboard. Each contained nails, buttons, paper clips, keys, hairpins, rusted coins, odd earrings, brooches, broken colourful glass, bangles, and old watches. He picked up these objects while walking back home from work. He emptied these cans onto the wooden floor and said, "Sit down! Sort everything in size, colour, and category. Call me when you're all done."

Neville, Pearl, Patsy, and I sorted these objects and placed them neatly in rows. My grandfather would examine each row. If they were all to his satisfaction, he'd say, "Well done!"

Then we threw it all back into the cans until the next time. There were times I felt like kicking those cans down the road.

Crafting

To keep us entertained on the weekends, Mumsie took us to the hardware store, where she bought large nails. We used them as knitting needles until we could knit without dropping any stitches. Once we became proficient, we graduated to the next level using real knitting needles and learned new patterns.

Maureen's craft was weaving colourful mats using discarded burlap sacks as matting. She would pull multi-coloured strips of material we collected from nearby clothing manufacturers neatly through the sack covering each hole.

Veronica did beautiful embroidery work.

Pearl loved dressmaking.

Patsy had a magnificent singing voice and helped weave.

My gift was knitting.

Neville took lessons in woodwork.

Each of us had to complete a project for gift-giving at Christmas.

Easter

As an Easter custom, Mumsie always made pickled fish by frying it, then covering it with curried pickled onion sauce. We enjoyed the meal with hot cross buns.

One Easter weekend, Mumsie had a severe angina attack, and the ambulance transported her to a nearby hospital. My father took charge of the Easter dinner. He descaled, cleaned, and chopped the fish into chunks. He then placed the carrots, potatoes, onions, parsley, and thyme on the table and said, "Wash and peel the vegetables, chop the parsley and the thyme."

We looked on in dismay as he filled a large pot with water, then added the chunks of fish and vegetables before placing the pot on the stove. We watched as the lid on the pot danced and the water boiled over, splashing onto the stove as the stew cooked.

We sat at the table. My father filled our plates with the fish stew, and Maureen handed us our plates. We tried our best to remove the bones as we ate.

I cried, "This is not how Mumsie makes pickled fish!"

My father replied, "You are fortunate to have a warm meal. Starving children in Soweto would be happy to have this meal."

Maureen and Veronica, who were expected to set an example, remained silent.

After Mumsie got discharged from the hospital, she could not return to work for a long time.

So, my father became the sole provider. As a result, there were times we ate stale bread soaked in water, sprinkled with sugar, or drizzled with condensed milk.

Mumsie's cousin, Aunt Kitty, and her husband, Uncle Me-Mo, owned an Italian Delicatessen in an upper-middle-class Italian neighbour-hood. Once a month, Aunt Kitty would bring a couple of brown paper bags filled with chicken carcasses for Mumsie to make soup, and a variety of off-cuts from the cold cuts, cheese, and Italian sausages. We looked forward to her visits and to munching on those morsels with gusto.

1948 – Setting the Foundation of Apartheid

At nine years old, I vaguely remember the hullabaloo when the National Party defeated General Smuts of the United Party. Daniel Francois D. F. Malan became prime minister of South Africa, setting the foundation of Apartheid in motion, requiring people to identify as one of six distinct racial groups: White, Coloured, Indian, Black, Muslim, and Other. This act broke up families and created a generation of bigots.

Before we moved to our new home, there were secret meetings with the authorities and my parents. After these meetings, they examined our hair facial features and textures to distinguish which racial group we best fit, i.e., black coloured or white. Some close relatives were classified as white and moved into different areas.

As told by Mumsie, "In 1937, at the time of King George the VI's coronation, 159 hectares with 553 stands located in the West Rand, a suburb of Johannesburg, were allotted for a housing project. The government built 730 homes on the land designated to accommodate People of Colour. The government then moved those they considered coloured with earnings over thirty dollars a month into the newly-built suburb named Coronationville."

My parents told us that we were lucky to be chosen for relocation to Coronationville as soon as the government completed the allotted building project.

Reclassification

Aunt Fiona and Uncle Theo, Mumsie's relations, now lived in an upscale neighbourhood. Mumsie and Aunt Fiona got into a bitter argument. Aunt Fiona said, "Maybe I should put these kids in bleach water."

Aghast, Mumsie scolded her, "God will punish you, Fiona, for being prejudiced toward your children."

From then on, we visited with our cousins after sunset so their neighbours would not become suspicious.

A family friend dropped Pearl and me off at the gate of Aunt Fiona's house at dusk a week before Christmas. As we ran up the poorly lit driveway, we were terrified when the neighbour's dog started barking, and the lights shone onto the driveway. Just then, thank God, Aunt Fiona opened the front door and quickly ushered us inside. Our cousins were delighted to see us as they came running down the staircase to greet us. Aunt Fiona had set the dining table with festive decorations and delicious food. As usual, there were rancid walnuts that we were prepared to empty into the paper bags we had in our overnight bag. We spent the weekend quietly playing dominos with the boys or cutting out paper dolls in the bedroom upstairs with the girls. We were fascinated with Priscilla's Drink and Wet doll.

A month later, when Patsy and I visited Aunt Fiona, the neighbour's dog scaled the fence, attacked us, and almost tore Patsy's eye out. The neighbour called his dog off but did not assess the damage that his dog caused. Patsy received three stitches to the inner corner of her right eye. I received long scratches to my arms to get the beast off my sister. Priscilla felt sorry for Patsy and gifted her the doll. That was our last overnight visit with our cousins.

Chapter Three

1948 – Moving Day

The long-awaited moving day finally arrived; we sat on the donkey cart, each with our thoughts as we bade farewell to our neighbours. We cried as the cart passed Charlie's grocery store, the school, the church and the cemetery. Although saddened, I looked forward to making new friends. As the donkeys moved onto the main road, I recalled the royal visit as I listened to the mules trotting.

Coronationville

On arrival at our new home, there was a frenzy of activity, as mounds of black soil, piles of red brick, steel poles, and large rolls of mesh wire fencing lay everywhere. Men were busy working as trucks moved up and down the street, unloading their building supplies.

There were no visible signs of paved roads or street signs. My father asked one of the men where 22 Franklin Street would be. He pointed to the red-brick semi-detached house. We jumped off the donkey cart and ran up the mound of dirt onto the front verandah.

As our father opened the front door, we wanted to be the first to enter our new home. A door led into a more spacious kitchen than the tiny kitchen with its sand-packed floor we left behind.

Entering the kitchen to the right stood a brand-new coal stove. Adjacent to the furnace was a large hot water tank. Leading off from the kitchen's left side were three bedrooms, a bathroom with a large bathtub, and a washbasin with faucets, including hot and cold running water, which we had never seen the likes of before.

Close to a built-in cement cupboard was the door leading to the back verandah. On one side stood a sink for washing dishes. Directly opposite was a toilet, which we did not have to share with the neighbours. In the backyard stood a freestanding red brick shed, large enough to store two bags of coal and a cord of wood.

Outside, the hustle and bustle continued. More families were simultaneously moving into the area. Children excitedly ran up and down the mounds of soil, getting in the way of the workers. Mumsie immediately summoned us into the house and directed us toward the end bedroom, saying, "Stay in the room until I call you for supper."

Inquisitively, we ran to the window and watched the men at work.

Once seated around the table, my father said a prayer of gratitude for our new home. Supper consisted of a bun stuffed with ground beef that Mumsie had packed before moving, followed by a cup of coffee.

After supper, my father announced that we were old enough to know the rent of our home would be twenty shillings a month. He earned a hundred shillings ($125) a month. Mumsie's wage was considerably less. With eight mouths to feed, new beds, drapes, coal, and wood to be bought, and bus fare and rent to be paid, my eldest sister, Maureen, would leave school and join Mumsie in working at the garment factory to help make ends meet.

Veronica was assigned to oversee the rest of us after school at age fifteen. We each had our chores to do. Veronica did her best to keep us under control, prompting us to finish our homework before venturing out to play. Some of us came home late from school but managed to complete our chores just before the working force, especially our parents, arrived home.

All the homes on our street were now fully occupied by people from different areas of Johannesburg. As kids, we were eager to make new friends. We played hopscotch, hide and seek, jump rope, marbles, and a host of other games in the street. I always got into trouble trying to protect my siblings from bullies who teased or tugged their hair.

New Friends and Neighbours

One of the children in the neighbourhood owned a bike we took turns riding. When my turn came, I could hardly wait to get going. As I sped downhill, the bicycle's chain came undone, and I headed straight toward a fence covered with lovely pink roses. As I landed head-first into the bush, I smelled the roses and screamed as the pain from the thorns ripped at my arms.

The owner of the rose bushes, Mrs. Van-Buren, a well-endowed woman with skinny eyebrows, had been watching us from her kitchen window. She charged out her front door, yelling, "You ruined my prize roses! I will be over to see your mother as soon as she comes home."

Everybody scattered off to their homes with a look of dread as Mrs. Van-Buren scolded and wagged her finger at us. I limped home with my clothes torn and legs bloodied.

Veronica cut up vegetables in preparation for dinner as we charged through the front door. When she saw me all bloodied and torn, it looked like she was ready to pass out. After relaying the story to her, looking squeamish, she said, "You better wash up and get those clothes out of sight. As soon as I let you out of the house, you'll get into trouble."

After the scratches were cleaned and plastered, she ushered us into the room and told us to remain there until our parents arrived.

Mumsie hardly had time to hang up her jacket before Mrs. Van-Buren came banging on the door, yelling, "McCrae! Your girls should not be riding boys' bikes and running wild after school. Come and look at how your daughter destroyed my prize roses."

Mumsie glanced at Veronica, who tearfully said, "They're in the room."

We were summoned out to apologize to Mrs. Van-Buren. With sorrowful eyes, we said, "We're sorry."

"Your father and I will deal with you after supper," said Mumsie.

We sat in silence during supper. Later, our parents scolded us for being disobedient. Feeling sorry for myself, I sulked for the rest of the evening.

The following day, Veronica told us to stay indoors and play dominos. A few friends asked if they could join us. One of them had celebrated his birthday and wanted to show us the kaleidoscope he was gifted. Reluctantly, Veronica agreed if we behaved. We were all fascinated and wanted to view the colourful pieces of glass as they swirled into different shapes.

During this time, there was much talk on the radio about artificial satellites. Rumour had it that a foreign object was spotted in the sky that might have had "little green men" aboard from other planets who could invade the world.

We all took turns with the kaleidoscope when somebody dropped it before passing it on to me. When I leaned my head back and lifted the tube with my eyes wide open, a piece of broken glass dropped into my eye. A neighbour drove Veronica and me to the nearby hospital. The doctor examined my eye, turned to Veronica, and said, "She has a foreign object in her eye."

On hearing the phrase "foreign object," my imagination kicked into high gear, thinking about little green men from another planet that was in my eye. Hysterical, I let out a blood-curling scream, "Get them out of my eye!"

The doctor calmed me down and assured me that there were no little green men in my eye. With the object removed and my eye bandaged, we headed home, knowing that we had more explaining to do when my parents arrived home.

Designated Areas

The appointed area we now lived in was growing by leaps and bounds. The council had strict rules for renting: no Muslims, Indians, Blacks, or Asians were allowed to live in the designated area.

It was classified as a Coloured township. A new community center, library, and churches were built. Gardens were springing up all around. Clubs were formed, giving us a feeling of pride in our new surroundings.

Rations

On the first Thursday of each month, we walked four miles after school to the council office, located in Sophiatown, a suburb of the City of Johannesburg. It was a parcel of land previously owned by Blacks and now zoned exclusively for whites and renamed Triomf. There, we collected our allotted rations of two margarine pounds and four bags of powdered milk. Occasionally, we received a large tub of peanut butter.

With Maureen now gainfully employed, Mumsie could buy a few home essentials on a layaway plan. There were no street signs posted yet, and because all red-brick homes looked alike at times, we could not identify our house. Mumsie bought the most beautiful emerald green velvet material to sew new drapes on her ancient Singer sewing machine. Using the foot treadle, we were allowed to hold the bobbin down while she wound the thread onto it. These drapes not only served as a window covering to keep the draft out but were used to distinguishing our home from the rest.

A mile from Coronationville, where we now lived, was Western Native Township, including Newclare Township. Here, residents were evacuated from their homes without proper planning for relocation. Most residents were Zulus, Bantus, and other Black tribes whose ancestors lived on the land for generations. When reclassification laws were enacted, they were officially derogatorily classified as "kaffirs" (a racist slur). They were moved into rural areas and forced to work on farms.

They were angry toward the government and hostile toward those moving into the newly built area. In retaliation, they waited until nightfall to storm into our occupied territory by smashing windows and setting fire to many businesses. We had dinner before dark, locked the doors, turned off the lights, and sat quietly in fear as we watched shadows pass by our windows. When we thought it was safe, we crawled into bed, but sleep did not come easy.

We lost touch with many of our old neighbours in Vrededorp and reconnected with others as we entered adult life. We learned they were scattered and moved to different areas. Some moved to Lenasia, designated an Indian suburb. The Muslims moved to Albertville; others with lesser earnings moved to Alexandria Township. Most merchants chose to remain in Vrededorp. Caucasians were relocated to Triomf.

Chapter Four

Pitfalls and Misbehaviour

Attending a new segregated school within walking distance from Newclare Township. We were stoned to and back from school by Zulu people and had to be creative in finding ways to avoid pitfalls through alleys and shortcuts. It was terrifying when big Zulu men carrying gnarled sticks surrounded the school, threatening to burn it down. During such times of unrest, the police squad cars transported us home.

Police raided the Zulu and Bantu homes that were not yet evacuated in search of illegal drugs or brewing liquor, referred to as "Kaffir Beer" or "KB." This beer was a concoction of fermented corn stored in large aluminum barrels sealed and buried underground. The natural ingredients used in the beer gave it a pinkish hue, and it had a distinct odour. We witnessed the police dig out the barrels and pour their contents onto the road. The stench permeated our nostrils.

The school had a riot of smells, and chalk dust billowed from blackboard erasers as we pounded them on the outside walls. A whiff of urine from someone accursed with a weak bladder. Boys tied the ribbons from our plaits onto the back of our desks, restricting our movements. Teachers inspected our fingernails for grime and the neatness of our tunics, shirts, ties, and polished shoes. These were the school's rules.

Boys crowded behind toilet buildings, tingling with wickedness. An appointee watched for any sign of teachers in sight while lighting up a twist of brown paper stuffed with tobacco gathered from cigarette butts. Taking drags in turn from the stuffed cigarette, they gagged, spat, and coughed. Eyes watering, they tried looking grown up as they stumbled back to class.

The principal, Mr. Johnstone, often sniffed out their secret, and the boys were lined up and made to bend over, touching their toes. Then the thin cane would come down, administering six rapid strokes on their rear ends in full view of the class. Of course, some would don two pairs of pants to lessen the pain, but Mr. Johnstone was wise to this trick and examined their posteriors before swiftly bringing down the cane.

For misbehaving in class, the culprits stood in the corner with dunce caps on their heads. A constant disruption notification to their parents would result in the leather strap at home. These strict disciplines allowed teachers to get on with teaching.

We had bullies at school. Marina, a tall, big-boned girl, picked on me for a few days, calling out, "Hey, Una, you get over here and tie my shoes," while her friends stood by laughing. After a few days of this humiliation, I decided I'd had enough! The next time Marina yelled, "Hey, you!" I ran toward her head down, hitting her full blast in her midriff. We both went down, resulting in a rolling, punching, hair-pulling brawl. She was getting the better of me, so I pulled her toward me, and bit her on her cheek. Everybody scattered. I ran home, sneaked through the backdoor into the bathroom, changed my clothes, and cleaned up without saying a word to anybody.

That evening after supper, my emotions ran high. Still wired while helping my mother with the laundry, there was a knock on the front door. As I opened it, lo and beheld, Marina stood with my teeth marks on her cheek, accompanied by her mother. Both of us had a lot of explaining to do.

After they left, Mumsie grabbed the wire hanger behind the bathroom door and whacked me several times. During the process, she repeatedly asked, "Do you want to be a dog? I'll build you a kennel in the backyard," she said.

"No, Mumsie," I whimpered, "she was bullying me."

Marina never demanded that I tie her shoes again.

A month later, I thought it would be fun playing hooky from school and joined the rabble-rousers, who said we were going to the forbidden blue dam for a swim. The dare excited me, even though I could not swim. When we arrived at the dam, the boys got rough and started pushing everybody into the water. I ran, but they caught up with me and threw me into the dam. I almost drowned. Luckily, one of the boys saw my distress and came to my rescue.

Word got to my parents. Furious, my father bellowed, "You could have drowned! I hope you learned your lesson, young lady."

Mumsie continued, "You will not be getting a new Easter dress, nor will you attend the service."

That night, I had a terrible nightmare of sinking to the bottom of the dam as I gasped for breath.

Entertainment

There were no seaside vacations; the best beaches were reserved for "whites only." Our community had a one-acre triangular-shaped playground containing a merry-go-round and four swings. The rest of the land was set aside as a soccer field. We tied pieces of off-cut material around our necks, got onto those swings, pumped our legs, raising the height of the swing, and as we jumped off, the wind caught under the material, billowing it out like wings. In our imagination, we were flying "like Superman." Alas! Some of us hit the ground hard.

Curious, we listened to gossip, took notes of the language of drunks, their arguments and fights, and mimicked their accents. We had ample material to keep ourselves entertained. We performed by creating live theatre and acting out scenes of what we heard and saw. We twisted our butts into pretzel shapes as we imitated Elvis Presley.

We raided the neighbours' pomegranate trees and ate fish and chips wrapped in newspaper—sometimes, I just bought the fish crumbs. We chewed on *biltong* (beef jerky), and we devoured delicious mango. The yellow juice ran down our wrists and arms. The boys climbed wild quince trees while we waited below for the fruit to drop, then we gathered them up to take home for our parents to bake. They were scrumptious with hot custard.

As part of our self-entertainment, we formed seven groups in teams with our friends, took off our shoes, and stamped our feet in the "red African soil," sending dust plumes into the air while imitating the *Indlamu*, the traditional Zulu warrior's war dance. We chanted unintelligently as we tried to outdo each other. I'm sure if any Zulu chief heard our gabble, he would have harpooned us. The red dust from the soil settled on our hair, faces, eyelashes, nostrils, and ears. *Oh! What fun we had*. It was priceless.

Exhausted, my brother, Neville, sisters Patsy and Pearl, and I headed home, looking like chimney sweepers from the red planet. I Made sure that we got home before the street lights turned on.

As we entered the kitchen door, Mumsie looked at us and called our father, "Percy, come and look at your children."

Our father smiled and looked amused. "Where have the lot of you been?'"

"Doing the Indlamu Zulu dance in the park," we boasted.

Both our parents laughed.

Mumsie said, "Clean up, and put all those soiled clothes in a separate basket."

Aunt Sarah's Introduction

After my biting and near-drowning incident, Mumsie decided to have Aunt Sarah move in with us. Aunt Sarah was a stubby, grey-haired, matronly old soul with a twinkle in her blue eyes.

The two of us did not see eye to eye. I received daily reprimands for being stubborn or wanting to express my opinion. There would be no mealy-mouthing your elders or questioning her hearsay. Whenever one of us children felt compelled to argue, and before we could utter a word, she'd say, "Bite your tongue!"

Shortly after Aunt Sarah arrived, Veronica joined Mumsie and Maureen in working at the garment factory.

At age eleven, I had my menses. Aunt Sarah hurriedly escorted me into the bedroom. After a long demonstration on using sanitary napkins, I was confused and afraid and asked, "Am I dying?"

She sternly replied, "No! You are not dying. Look at me and listen carefully to what I'm saying. Today, you have become a young lady. You will no longer participate in rough sports with boys and run wild. Boys will get you pregnant, and you will have a baby."

All this new information and restriction caused me to wail like a banshee. After Mumsie heard the news, I had another private conversation.

"This is to be kept a secret between us ladies. You will go through a twenty-eight-day cycle each month. If you miss a day, you must let me know immediately," she said.

Afterward, she handed me a hot cup of milk and told me to keep warm. I did not attend school the following day.

After school, my friends called to find out if I was sick and if I would come out to play.

Aunt Sarah said, "Una is not feeling well, and she will no longer be joining you in after-school games."

They were afraid of her and dared not ask further questions. I was vowed to secrecy.

Everything went off well for the first couple of months, but the following month, I was two days overdue. Concerned, jumpy, and ill-tempered, I anxiously waited for Mumsie to come home from work, but dinner was on the table before I could talk with her. We usually took turns in sharing the events of the day after dinner. When my turn came, I looked at Mumsie, hoping she would understand what I meant, when I nervously said, "Mumsie, I still did not get my parcel from the post office."

Baffled, Mumsie stared at me with a blank expression.

My brother Neville asked, "What parcel are you expecting from the post office?"

Mumsie excused us from the table. Once in the bedroom, I explained my predicament to her.

In the kitchen, my father and siblings waited with bated breath.

Mumsie, in her wisdom, explained, "Sally entered a competition through the newspaper and is anxiously waiting for the results."

Coal Rationing

During the winter of 1948, there was coal rationing in Johannesburg. The windows in our modest homes were all single-paned, and there was no central heating. With only a few cords of wood left in the shed to keep the fire burning, allowing us to cook, we gathered all of our worn-out old shoes, piled a few into the stove, then added paraffin oil (kerosene), setting it alight to keep us warm during the night. The burning of the leather plus the smell from the paraffin caused us to cough all night.

Our neighbour, Mr. Isaac, who worked on the city council, told my parents that to obtain our coal quota, we had to go down to the nearest train station to await the incoming morning train carrying the coal.

A group of neighbours hired a man with a donkey cart to transport us to the station. My parents assigned Pearl, Neville, and me to join the group.

The following morning, we packed a lunch of peanut butter sandwiches and three flasks of coffee before loading three large spades for shovelling coal onto the cart. Joining us were Mr. Isaac's daughters, Norma and Thora. Norma looked very fashionable, wearing a white angora sweater. Upon arrival at the station, we joined the long line-up, each receiving a sack to shovel our coal into. We waited in line for hours and soon devoured our lunch. Then, finally, we heard the chug-a-lug of the heavy-laden train as the wheels hit the rails.

Squeak! The train came to a halt. The side levers lowered, and the coal poured out in billowing clouds of black soot, almost suffocating us. *Clang! Clang!* Our spades echoed as everybody silently shovelled coal into their allotted bags. The older men helped us drag and lift the sacks onto the donkey cart. I noticed Norma's white angora sweater was now a dark shade of grey. We all looked like chimney sweepers, coughing, spitting, and blowing soot from our nostrils. Nobody said a word as we sat on our coal sacks, exhausted and hungry.

I looked forward to getting home and felt grateful knowing that Aunt Sarah would have a basin of hot water and sunlight soap ready for us to wash away the grime—and a hot bowl of soup ready to warm our bellies.

1950 – Johannesburg Evening News (The Rand Daily Mail)

Hendrik Verwoerd, the minister of native affairs, announced strict regulations of the Apartheid laws. There will be no mixing of segregated groups in churches or any other function, public or private. The government arrested those who spoke out against the Apartheid laws and placed them under house arrest: schoolteachers, businesspeople, students, doctors, and the ordinary men and women deemed suspects were held captive in their own homes and deprived of working to earn a living.

The government required them to report to police headquarters twice daily under police escort and restricted them to receiving two visitors a day, with approval from the authorities. The found suspect was tortured by inserting electric crawlers into their scrotum. Some were forced to jump from balconies ten storeys high.

At eleven years old, I, like many others, witnessed some house arrests in our neighbourhood and the hardship it caused for those families.

Space to Grow

As our family grew in age, and after long debates trying to convince the council that we needed more space to grow, our family moved into a free-standing three-bedroom house on 29 Bathurst Street, directly behind the Dutch Reformed church. We had a hundred-degree view of the library, recreation centre, Catholic church, and stores from our kitchen window.

By this time, Aunt Sarah had complete control of the household. We were busy as bumblebees, singing as we did our daily chores. There was no longer the smell of caustic soda or disinfectant in the house. Fab, a new washing powder, made its appearance on the market. I can still hear its slogan that was sung on the radio, "Fab-Fab-F.A.B. Just you, Fab, and you will see."

During springtime, a burst of pink and white blossoms adorned the fruit trees in the neighbourhood. The fragrance from the honeysuckle vines permeated the whole house during the summer months. A feeling of excitement, anticipation and new beginnings filled my being.

We also had a mulberry tree, which the children in the neighbourhood ransacked after school each day, descending when satiated. And a fig tree that bore large fruit bursting with succulent sweetness.

Our homes had sloped, corrugated zinc roofs, allowing objects to roll down slowly. Friends and boyfriends alike threw little stones onto the rooftop to signal that we were late for a date. The favourite pranks the boys played were wrapping string around a stone and tying it around the door handle by pulling the line. It sounded like someone was knocking on the door. These pranks irked my father.

Valentine's Day 1953

The doorbell rang. I opened the door to one of the church's male choir members holding a beautiful bouquet of red roses. He asked if my parents were home. I said, "Yes," and invited him into the living room.

Then I called out, "Mumsie, you have a visitor."

As soon as Maureen saw him, she ran into the bedroom and shut the door. Pearl and I were curious to know why the young man with the roses wanted to see my parents. We hid in the bedroom opposite the living room but left the door ajar so we could peek and eavesdrop on the conversation.

Once my parents were seated, he nervously introduced himself as David Abrahams and said, "Mr. and Mrs. McCrae, I've come to ask your permission to court your daughter Maureen."

We heard my father clear his throat before he spoke. We leaned closer toward the opening of the door, awaiting his answer.

My father asked David, "How do you know Maureen, young man? Where do you live, and what is your occupation?"

David replied, "My family and I attend the same church you do, sir. We live four blocks from the church."

My father then summoned Maureen to the living room.

Nervously she entered, twisting her long plaits.

Father asked Maureen, "How do you know David?"

She replied, "We attend the same Bible study class, Dad."

David anxiously asked, "Sir, may I give Maureen these roses for Valentine's Day?"

My father consented. Maureen smiled, accepted the roses, and thanked David.

"Place the roses in a vase of lukewarm water, Maureen, and come back," Mumsie said.

Once Maureen was seated, my father said, "I don't know you or your family. Before I decide, I would like to meet your parents."

David agreed, thanked my parents, and left. We quietly shut the door and pretended to do our homework. Later that evening, we noticed our parents in deep conversation with Maureen.

A year later, Maureen and David wed. David was a talented design carpenter and had decided that he wanted to be self-employed. David often had no income, and he liked to play the ponies (bet on horseracing). Maureen worked at a large warehouse. Life was not easy.

She bore three sons and two daughters. Mumsie helped whenever she could. Maureen and David remained married for sixty years before he passed on in his late eighties. Their children grew into talented adults who are working in the arts.

Chapter Five

Joining the Workforce

A year later, I joined my mother and two sisters at Ducksons' Menswear Clothing Manufacturer.

My introduction to the factory was a rude awakening.

Monday to Friday morning, we clocked in at 7:30 a.m. and out at 5:30 p.m. There were deductions of wages for those who clocked in late. We did piecework. If you were sewing sleeves onto a jacket, it would roll along a conveyer belt. By the time the next piece came moving along, you had better be ready for the next sleeve.

Winnie, the forelady, patrolled the aisles, keeping an eye on the slackers that jammed up the conveyer belt. At 10 a.m., a loud buzzer would sound, and everybody on the machines got up and headed toward the lavatories (toilets) to wait in line. The alarm to get back to work would often blast before many of us reached the toilets. For the first couple of weeks, I abided by the rule. During my second week of employment, I had had enough of being treated like a herd animal.

The following Monday, when the alarm sounded, I sat at my machine while my fellow workers ran to get to the lavatories on time. After everybody got back to their machines, I got up and headed in the direction from which they came.

The foreman Mr. Beaty immediately spotted me and yelled, "Hey, you! Where do you think you are going?" I inhaled then exhaled before I yelled back, "My bladder is not controlled by an alarm bell. So, I'm going to the lavatory now!"

A back-and-forth shouting match erupted between the foreman and me. In rapid succession, he spewed out profane language against me.

I confronted him and yelled, "I'm not an animal, and I refuse to work under these conditions. I'm quitting this shameful job, and you can shove that measly paycheck."

I looked over to where Mumsie and my sisters sat in disbelief.

The foreman was livid. The veins stood out on his neck. Furious, he fired me, my mother, and my two sisters on the spot.

Veronica found new employment at Carolla's Upholstery as a seamstress the following week.

New Employment

Two weeks later, Progress Clothing Manufacturers employed Maureen, Mumsie, and me. This company was a much happier environment; there were no restrictions on using the lavatories. Every morning, as soon as the machines started up, Walter, the head of our working team, who had an excellent baritone voice, would belt out one of the popular hit songs, and everybody followed in tandem.

His favourite song "The Great Pretender."[2] The choir sang above the noise of the machines while the conveyor belts kept moving along.

2   The Platters, 'The Great Pretender'
     Writer: Buck Ram
     Producer: Ram
     Released: Dec. '55, Mercury
     24 weeks; No. 1

Mr. Goldberg, the owner, whom we referred to as "Papa," walked the floor smiling as we sang. At the end of the year, we all received a healthy bonus in our pay envelopes in appreciation for outstanding work performed.

Joan Campbell, a fellow employee and friend, occupied the chair opposite mine at the machines. We giggled when Mrs. Moyce, a co-worker, frantically searched for her spectacles while they sat on the top of her head. Joan and I had many eye conversations while at work.

Solly, the boss's son, always sat at the front desk, looking very bored as he squeezed the zits on his face. He smiled whenever we passed by him. One day, as we sat outside during our lunch break, he approached us and started a conversation.

"Hello, are you sisters?" he asked.

Surprised, we answered, "No, we're not sisters; we're friends."

Joan introduced herself, then, referring to me, she said, "Her name is Una."

The three of us became buddies, meeting at a secluded spot during our lunch breaks. We learned about his lifestyle and eating habits—matzah, chicken livers, and Passover. In exchange, he discovered a few details about our way of life.

Solly took charge of the first aid box and handed out aspirin when needed. One day, he asked if I would like to handle the box. Naturally, I welcomed this sidetrack away from the machines and immediately said, "Yes, I would love to."

Solly smiled and showed me where he hid the key to the box.

Joan said, "I think he likes you, Una." We started flirting with him whenever he made an appearance, and we rolled our eyes at each other to indicate that he was around.

Word got out that we were secretly meeting with Solly during lunch. We were having a lovely time one afternoon when Mumsie appeared on the scene, addressing the three of us. "Do you want to be arrested and go to prison?" She scolded.

After the incident, the three of us kept our distance but exchanged glances. We looked forward to coming to work; it kept our adrenaline pumping. Mumsie kept a watchful eye on the situation, and she was happy to learn that Solly was getting married a year later.

Garment Workers' Union

Pamphlets circulated indicating a workers' union had formed in protest of unfair wages and the despicable treatment of factory workers. A rally was scheduled to be held in the city. Thousands of workers attended the first workers' union rally. There were people in trees, balconies, and nearby businesses listening and observing. The police presence kept the large crowd in control.

Onstage, the first speaker spoke about forming a garment workers' union. Loud applause rang out.

The second speaker spoke about fair wage agreements. People began chanting.

"Yes, fair wages! We all pay the same price for bread, regardless of how much we earn. Fair wages for all, fair wages for all!"

Suddenly, all hell broke loose. The police moved in with brutal force, whipping everybody on the site. Gunshots rang out, and chaos erupted. People screamed and ran, trying to avoid being killed. Some got trampled in the stampede as they tried to find their relatives.

I ran down back alleys, hoping my family members were out of harm's way. Fortunately for us, a sprained ankle and a lost purse was the worst injury out of our group.

The following day, Springbok Radio announced that many people had lost their lives. Despite all the violence, the garment workers' union prevailed.

Bloody Encounter

Patsy and I arrived home late from a concert, all bloodied and bruised, during this period. In shock, my mother asked, "What happened to the two of you?"

With tears streaming down our faces, we tried speaking at once. Finally, I blurted out, "The conductor on the bus tried to prevent us from boarding because Fatima, our Indian friend who accompanied us, was dark-skinned.

The conductor asked, 'What are you doing with this Coolie?" Infuriated at his demeaning and unnecessary remark, I countered and said, 'Maybe your sister is a Coolie.' He pushed Patsy and she fell onto the person in the seat in front of us. He slapped me across my face. I exploded, took off my shoe, and hit him on his head with the heel of my shoe. There was blood everywhere. Chaos broke out with a free-for-all, punching and pulling. We got off the bus at the next stop, before the police arrived."

Aghast, my father scolded, "Clean up and come to the table. We will discuss this matter after dinner."

We sat in silence at the table, eating. I still had more fights in me. I slowly felt all the injustice welling up in my throat, preventing me from swallowing my food. This feeling propelled me from my chair.

I yelled out, "Dammit! When will this end?"

My brother, Neville, stopped eating. His fork was in hand, midway to his mouth. He tried saying something, but no words formed. All eyes looked at me, waiting for my subsequent reaction, which did not take long.

I shouted, "I'm going to stand up and fight!"

"Enough! I don't want you to stoop to their level," my father scolded.

I thought, *what level do I have?* and phrased the word l-e-v-e-l under my breath.

"Let's bow our heads in prayer and ask for protection," my father said.

We bowed our heads as he prayed. My mind was still on the bus.

Each weekday, after supper, we listened to the spine-chilling radio show *The Creaking Door* on Lux Radio or Bristol Myers Radio Theatre. Our hyperactive imaginations worked overtime as we listened to every word and eerie sound. After the series, none of us dared venture outside after dark to bring in the coal.

Our neighbours, the Leckays, owned a television, and we were lucky to be invited to watch early shows on Friday afternoons. On one such occasion, the television was on when Mr. Leckay left the room. I heard a catchy tune called, Roll Me Over in the Clover.[3] Later, feeling happy, bouncing around the kitchen, my ponytail bobbing, I sang, roll me over, roll me over in the clover…

Aunt Sarah rushed over and slapped me across the face. Stunned, my jingle stopped, and my debut abruptly ended.

"Where did you hear that song?" Aunt Sarah asked.

Knowing that slap meant something was wrong, and not wanting to say I heard it on the television at the Leckays', I said, "I heard it over the radio."

"I never want to hear you sing that song again," Aunt Sarah scolded.

Indignant, I yelled, "What did I do wrong by dancing and singing? That's why I don't like staying home. There's always something wrong!" I howled.

Sobbing, I ran to the bedroom and slammed the door so hard that an ornament from the shelving above the door crashed to the floor and shattered.

---

3   Provided to YouTube by Zebralution GmbH Roll Me over the Clover (Remastered) · Rusty Warren
    Golden Selection Music Publisher: Jubilee Records

Aunt Sarah yelled, "You get out here, young lady, and clean up the mess!"

When I opened the door and saw the glass fragments, I was so angry that I felt like pulverizing them. Growing up in a small village, the neighbours noted everything you did. They counted the months from the day you married to the day you gave birth. Being chaste was of the utmost importance. We stayed home until we got married. Those who moved out alone or fell pregnant before marriage were considered sluts. If a young man got a girl pregnant, her father quickly marched them to the altar.

We attended Bible studies, choir practice, the youth guild, and morning and evening services on Sundays.

We were read: For you, my brothers and sisters were called to be free[4] (Galatians 5:13-15, NIV).

The last sentence put fear into me. I recalled biting Marina and also had frequent flashbacks of being molested.

I never let myself become too close to my sisters or anybody else. I feared I might slip up and reveal my secret of being molested and that I would be labelled a slut. I always found something outside the house to keep me busy: sports, dancing, or knitting clubs.

Cinema

We were allowed to attend the matinee shows at the only cinema, called the Reno. Located in Newclare Township, a fifteen-minute walk from where we lived. The owner, a Jewish man whom we referred to as "Die Jood." *A Jewish man* stood outside the cinema, cracking his long black leather whip to keep things in order.

He told the younger children, "If you move forward to the front-row seats, you will see the movie first."

4   http://www. christianity.com/bible/niv

In the movies, actors and actresses mostly held hands; there were no passionate kisses. My friend Gloria and I heard about an upcoming movie called *April Love*, starring Shirley Jones and Pat Boone, in which Pat Boone was the first actor to kiss his co-star in a motion picture.

We skipped Bible studies and attempted to go to the cinema to see the movie. At the box office, my cousin Shirley was working. She smiled, looked around, gave us our tickets, and said, "Sit in the upper seats against the wall, close to the exit door."

At the end of the movie, everybody stood up and cheered. We quickly left the cinema and ran back to the church as some of the older boys walked to their cars.

"Where have the two of you been? Some big romance going on?" Sylvan, one of the leaders, asked.

Gloria and I sheepishly looked at each other. Then I finally asked, "What do you mean by romance?"

Sylvan replied, "Too bad you were not here. I will let you know next time."

The following week at bible study, we read: Therefore, shall a man leave his father and his mother and cleave unto his wife: and they shall be one flesh[5] (Genesis 2:24, NIV).

Sylvan gave us our first explanation of procreation, or *sex*, in simple terms: the intrinsic and powerful meaning of one-flesh union. When Adam and Eve lay down and became one flesh, they created life. Adam and Eve begat Cain and Abel.

I now had my answer to why Aunt Sarah slapped me when I sang, "Roll me Over in the ... clover."

I asked Sylvan again what was meant by romance. Sylvan explained it was the feeling of physical attraction between males and females: eye

5   http://www.christianity.com/bible/niv

contact, electrical sparks when you touch, and warm fuzzy feelings that either party could misinterpret as love.

After bible study, a few girls were curious about that warm fuzzy feeling. We giggled when speaking of it, and Mariana said, "If any of you experience that feeling, let me know."

Gloria said, "I got an electric shock once when I touched the socket on the wall."

I said, "Yikes, my dad called someone to fix the wiring dangling loosely in the backyard. The man was inexperienced and touched the wires. The shock threw him across the yard." We had a good laugh as we carried on home.

I admired my sister Veronica's dark hair as it fell onto her shoulders, her obedience and patience as she sat doing exquisite embroidery work that she sold at Christmas Bazaars. She also had excellent penmanship.

Sisterly Love

During our conversations, she asked me, "Why don't you listen, Sally? I feel sorry for you when Dad punishes you."

I said, "I love dancing and just want to have some fun. Don't you?"

Looking forlorn, Veronica smiled and continued her embroidery work.

I could not help but notice her dentures. "Your dentures look good," I commented. "Do you remember how scary it was visiting the public dentist in the city? We stood in line for hours before we were seated and handed a number. The nurse made her rounds, injecting our gums with Novocain. Our noses numbed while we nervously waited. We heard the teeth of those who entered before us dropping, *cling! Cling!* into the metal buckets.

"I will never forget the day you were so infuriated during your dental visit that you decided to have all your teeth extracted in one sitting, then boarded the bus home with your mouth filled with bloody cotton wool. You were lucky you made it home before you fainted at the front door. We were all concerned when the doctor recommended that you stay in bed for the next few days."

A year after, Veronica celebrated her eighteenth birthday. Alfred Constable, ten years her senior, came to ask my father for her hand in marriage. Although I was excited when she asked me to be her bridesmaid, I felt sad that she was getting married to an older man.

Veronica was a seamstress and sewed most of her clothes. I loved the beautiful cape coats she wore and the matching pillbox hats Mumsie made to match her outfits.

Two years after her marriage, she gave birth to her daughter, Ingrid. Five years later, Veronica was pregnant and ecstatic, hoping it would be a boy. But it was not to be—the baby boy was stillborn. Devastated, they waited two and half years before conceiving again.

At age twenty-nine, Veronica gave birth to a healthy baby girl named Oreen. Six months after giving birth, Veronica was diagnosed with pneumonia and hospitalized. After being given a clean bill of health and being discharged a week later, she died of a massive heart attack. We were all shocked and heartbroken by her sudden death and for her two young children, ages eight and six months old.

Veronica's death was the first in our family. As was the custom, we mourned her death by wearing black dresses and stockings for three months. My father and brother Neville wore black armbands. We were all saddened that Veronica died at such a young age, before she could experience the joy of watching her children and grandchildren grow into adult life. At times, I would get a whiff of the top notes of her favourite perfume, White Shoulders, with jasmine, gardenia, orange blossom, and sandalwood.

Chapter Six

Family Secrets Revealed

I met and befriended a boy named John McCrae, who had the same last name as ours. Excited, I invited him to our home to meet my family.

I introduced him to Mumsie, "This is John McCrae," and waited for her reaction. Mumsie greeted John, went into the kitchen, and returned with tea and scones on a tray, followed by my father.

My father greeted John and said, "So, you have the same last name as us, McCrae. What is your father's name, John? And where do you live?"

John nervously squirmed in the chair and replied, "My father's name is Basil, and we live in Mayfair."

After small talk, John said, "I'm working as an apprentice in my uncle's business. We're repairing Mr. Jones's roof across the road."

John glanced at his watch and said, "Thank you for the tea and scones, Mrs. McCrae. My break is over. I have to get back to work."

After John left, my parents gathered all of my siblings into the living room, then all of our family's skeletons came tumbling out of the closet.

My mother looked at me and said, "I want you to stay away from John. He might be related to you."

Before I could retaliate, she continued, "You children might have wondered why you never see your grandparents from your father's side or why we never talk about them."

We waited in anticipation.

My father took over the conversation. "My father and your grandfather's parents were from Scotland. My father was a womanizer in his young days. He married my mother at a young age but continued sowing his wild oats. They later divorced after my mother learned about his two illegitimate children. Later, my mother learned he had several marriages. She lost touch with him, and we've had no further contact."

Mumsie pointed to a large, framed photograph hanging on the living room wall of a woman who looked very serene, with long, dark braided hair. "This is my mother, your grandmother. Her name is Helena Buckley. She was born in Jamestown on the island of St. Helena, far, far away from here," she said.

I always wondered who the woman in the photograph was.

When Maureen and Veronica did not seem surprised, my younger siblings and I looked at each other questionably.

Mumsie continued, "When the government started reclassifying everybody, I did not want them to separate us because we differ in the colour of our skin. As you noticed, some family members chose to be reclassified and moved."

This revelation slowly permeated my being, and I became more curious as time went on.

I questioned Aunt Sarah, my grandmother's sister, about St. Helena.

She revealed that in 1871, she and my grandmother joined more than two thousand St. Helenians (along with their employers) who ventured away from the island across the Atlantic Ocean toward the Cape to find a better life.

Upon hearing all this new information, and the changes happening around me, I began to look at things through a different lens.

Visiting my now reclassified relatives, I realized the added benefits they received, including the many times they pretended not to know us in public places. When invited to their homes, they'd ask, "Do you have a boyfriend? I hope he does not have naughty hair."

My father's sister, Aunty Sophie, and her husband, Andrew Merkel, were childless. They lived in a fancy house in Mayfair. She would frequently ask my mother and me over for tea. While serving tea, she would entice me to live with her. She would show me the spare bedroom and point out all the advantages I would have. I was mildly impressed but hesitated, knowing I would be her only child and I would miss my parents and siblings.

Mumsie, the family matriarch, was always ready to lend an ear to whoever needed someone to listen to their problems. I recall one of her regular visitors who greeted my mother, "Hello, Mrs. McCrae. You know, McCrae, if it's not one thing, it's another, but there's always a thing."

My sibling and I secretly nicknamed her Mrs. Thingy-Me-Bob (TMB).

One day, Patsy slipped up. When Mrs. TMB knocked on the front door, she innocently announced, "Mumsie, Mrs. Thingy-Me-Bob is here."

Before my mother opened the door, she ushered us into the backroom. Mumsie later scolded us for being disrespectful toward our elders. Unlike today, we were not allowed to sit in on such conversations. The only time we mingled with our elders was once a month, during prayer meetings held at our home with three other families.

Once the pastor said prayers, the children left the room and gathered in the back bedroom until the meeting was over.

My elder sisters served the visitors tea in Royal Albert Old Country Rose cups, along with Mumsie's scrumptious pastries. The cups and saucers she inherited were reserved for special occasions.

The children received hot mugs of either Milo or Ovaltine. Afterward, my sisters and I carefully washed the fine China and packed it in the cupboard until next time.

A few pastors met at our home to discuss the government's intention to ban all church gatherings between Black, white, and coloured congregations. I was too busy having fun to understand the full impact of the Apartheid laws and their effect on my life in later years.

1950 – The Amendment of the Immorality Act

Apartheid and the Immorality Act forbade any intercourse or marriage between whites, Blacks, mixed-race, or Asian people. Individuals found guilty of such an offence would be liable on conviction to imprisonment for five years.

Before the Immorality Act became law, many women gave birth in interracial relationships or marriages. Many of these parents abandoned their children for fear of being implicated, and their children found refuge at St. Joseph's Children's Home in nearby Sophiatown.

The Foundlings

One day, we heard cries coming from the churchyard behind our backyard fence. Mumsie and I decided to investigate. We were shocked to discover two children, a little boy and girl huddled together in a wheelbarrow. The girl seemed to be about four years old and the boy was approximately two years old.

Mumsie asked the girl, "What is your name?"

She replied, "Arlette."

"And his name?" Mumsie asked, pointing to the boy.

With tears streaming down her face, she tugged at her unkempt blonde curly locks and replied, "Tony."

"Where is your mother?" Mumsie asked.

Whimpering, Arlette said, "I don't know."

Little Tony looked on with sad amber eyes and a runny nose. Both of them looked petrified as they clung to each other. Mumsie took pity on Arlette and Tony. We took them home and bathed and fed them.

For the next couple of days, little Tony crouched in a corner, sucking his thumb. Arlette adapted more easily. In fear of what would become of them if she reported it to the authorities, my parents decided to keep them. They became an addition to our family for the next year until my parents figured out their next step.

A year later, a friend of Mumsie adopted Arlette. I remember how traumatic it was when she cried and held onto my skirt, refusing to let go. When her adopted parents came to take her to her new home, we cried ourselves to sleep that night.

My cousin Millie adopted Tony later that same year. We kept in touch with them over the years. Fortunately, both matured into happy, stable adults.

1955 – The First Kiss

I found my first French kiss disgusting and repulsive. I promptly ran straight home to the bathroom, brushed my teeth, and gave my mouth a thorough rinse with Dettol. Reaching for my stash of charcoal, I polished my teeth until they shone. I hoped nobody noticed the extra time I spent in the bathroom.

The following weekend, the Catholic church held its annual dance at the recreation centre, just steps away from our home. I knew Ronnie, the kisser, would be in attendance, and I was not allowed to attend the function, but my curiosity got the better of me. I lied to my father, telling him I was going to the store. Unbeknown to me, my father stood at the kitchen window in full view of the recreation centre and the stores, watching me.

I slipped into the hall. Ronnie saw me and waved just as the band struck up with the song "It's Cherry Pink and Apple Blossom White." As we stepped onto the dance floor, Ronnie's friend ran over to let us know my father was looking for me at the front door.

I tried ducking through the side door, but my father was waiting, leather strap in hand. He gave me a licking in full view of everybody. Embarrassed and stubborn, I walked tall, refusing to let out a whimper until we reached home. My siblings scattered when they heard my wails as I ran into the house. Both my parents chastised me for being disobedient.

Mumsie asked, "When are you going to stop being so stubborn? Why can't you be like your brother and sisters? They never give us any problems."

I thought to myself; They're *so boring*.

I replied, "I can't go anywhere. All my friends were there. It was just one dance."

Feeling sorry, I crawled into bed, fully dressed, shoes and all.

I lay in bed, wondering why my siblings were so immutable. Maybe there was something wrong with me. I was not living by the rule of the bible[6] (Exodus 20:12, NIV).

Two months after the dance, Ronnie celebrated his eighteenth birthday. We met at a park under a large tree next to Mrs. Dickson's house, facing her kitchen window. As we embraced, I felt that warm fuzzy feeling. Mrs. Dickson flung open her kitchen window and doused us with a bucket of cold water. Startled and dripping wet, we scattered.

My first thought was, *Oh, shit! How will I explain why I look like a drowned rat when I get home?* I wished him a happy birthday and said, "I've got to go."

6   http://www.christianity.com/bible/niv

My hair and blouse were still damp as I sneaked through the back door into the bedroom and changed.

The next time I saw Ronnie, he said, "I think I'm falling in love with you. I want to be the first to make love to you."

Taken aback, I felt uncomfortable and said, "My father would kill both of us if there were any lovemaking. Besides, you are Catholic, and I am a Methodist."

"You're teasing me," he said.

Ronnie was not happy with my answer or explanation. We parted on unfriendly terms.

The following week, Ronnie and his soccer team, the Falcons, were slated to play a Durban game, a six-hour drive from Johannesburg, and billeted to stay over the weekend.

After the game, there was still no contact between us. Wondering if Ronnie was still upset with me, one Sunday morning, I walked over to the store to buy the *Sunday Times* newspaper, hoping to see him there. The owner of the store was Catholic. I knew I had to wait in line until the Catholic service was over, and all the Catholics got their papers before I paid for mine.

I patiently waited, but there was no sign of him. A couple of months later, rumours began to circulate. Ronnie had met a girl in Durban, and she was pregnant. This was confirmed by a friend of his. Devastated, I avoided my friends. I did not want to talk about it. Ronnie and I avoided each other. Whenever I saw Ronnie waiting in line at the bus stop, I waited for the next bus. Ronnie soon wed and moved away, and I got over my disappointment.

The Year of Rock and Roll

We wore flared skirts with a crinoline that we starched to make the hemline stand out wider. I dipped mine in sugar water to make it stand out even wider. Metal figure belts were in fashion, and each time I wore that belt, Aunt Sarah asked, "Are you tying up your guts again? You better keep that belt fastened, young lady."

I hula hooped until I was dizzy while Aunt Sarah shook her head and looked on in dismay.

Up to this point, I was still wearing bobby socks. A month before my seventeenth birthday, Mumsie surprised me by saying, "You are now old enough to get out of those socks. But it's undignified for a young woman to go bare-legged, so I bought you a pair of nylons and a garter belt to hold them up."

Mumsie took the nylons out of the package. They were quite flimsy and had a black seam running straight down the back. I thought, "How on earth will they keep my legs warm?"

I tried them on. Oh, heavens! I could not get those seams to stay in a straight line. And I was afraid if I tugged, I'd ripped them. After wearing those nylons for a week, I felt naked, and I had no patience trying to keep those darn seams straight. I put them back into the drawer.

A couple of weeks later, feeling all grown up, I tried them on again, intending to walk down to my friend Elizabeth's home. As I neared the stores, a couple of boys were idly hanging around, smoking. Kingsley, one of the boys, said, "Wow! Look! She's wearing nylons." They whistled and said, "How about a date?"

Embarrassed, I turned around and ran back home. For a while, I kept switching back and forth between nylons and socks until I became familiar with wearing them.

Revival Services

Tent revival services were springing up in and around the neighbourhood. Curious, we attended many without our parents' knowledge. At times, the tents would be crowded, and we would peep through the tent holes at the frenzy of activity. There were lots of "Hallelujahs." The missionaries were performing miracles. People were falling to the ground proclaiming that they were healed. These services boggled our minds.

Mumsie found out about our little escapades and asked, "What were you doing in those tents?"

We replied excitedly, "People were being healed. One man said he was deaf, and the minister prayed, slapped his ear, and the man said he could hear for the first time."

"That is false!" Mumsie said, "Only Jesus can heal. I don't want you to put your feet into those tents again, do you hear me?"

"Yes, Mumsie," we replied. Of course, we still went.

A new sound of music was born when Elvis Presley shook, rattled, and rolled across the globe in his "Blue Suede Shoes," twisting his way into our hearts. He created a new genre of music known as rock n' roll, integrating blues, gospel, and country music.

Elvis portrayed the mixed-race son of a white rancher in the movie *Flaming Star*. His beautiful Kiowa Indigenous wife, played by Dolores Del Rio, a Mexican actress, was banned in South Africa.

My sisters and I laughed when we read an article in the newspaper about a woman in Stellenbosch in the Western Cape who destroyed her substantial collection of Nat King Cole's records when she learned he was Black. I thought, *How ridiculous.*

Neville rolled my father's cigarettes on a little rolling machine. At age thirteen, he stole one of my father's cigarettes. As punishment, my father put his fingers on a hot coal stove to set an example for all of us. Mumsie treated the blisters on Neville's two middle fingers by applying Vaseline to them. They took about ten days to heal. I recall Neville putting crickets into matchboxes and strategically placing them around the house. That night, the crickets chirped so loudly, and we had to find where he hid them so we could throw them back outside. My father was more annoyed than angry.

Grocery Shopping

Our family never owned a car; we travelled by train or bus into the city to do our major grocery shopping. We carried everything in brown paper bags since there was no plastic during this time. It was a total disaster when Maureen, Veronica, and I went shopping, and it unexpectedly rained, causing the bags to break.

While waiting for the bus, the canned food rolled, and whole fresh fish slipped and slid. We either laughed or cried as we wrapped those items in jackets, coats, scarves, or whatever bags we could salvage to transport our groceries home.

Fortunately, on a particular day, we travelled by bus, and we had a fifteen-minute walk home with our haul. When we arrived home, our clothes were damp and our hair dishevelled.

Mumsie said, "You poor children. I'm sorry you got caught in the downpour. Hurry! Change your clothes before you catch a cold."

We dried our hair and hung our wet clothes to dry; Mumsie had packed the groceries away and handed us a hot mug of cocoa.

Petty Apartheid Laws

At age sixteen, I learned about the political situation when churches were separated. Those of colour were not allowed entrance to theatres, restaurants, beaches, or parks. No sports competitions were allowed between different races. In the Orange Free State, Blacks were not allowed to walk on the same sidewalk as white people. They had to step aside and walk on the road.

"Whites Only," notices appeared in every conceivable place. Five seats in the back of city busses were allowed for those of colour. Regardless of whether the bus was empty, a person of colour had to wait for the next available bus.

Healthcare became regulated and ambulance services had to be specified. If you were a person of colour *and were lying dying* on the road after an accident, you would have to wait for a non-white ambulance to transport you to a non-white hospital.

The police hid in trees, peeked through windows, and followed those suspected of engaging in interracial relationships. They raided homes at night, smashing doors and inspecting bed linen and underwear, confiscating anything they thought could be used as evidence. Those found guilty of violating the prohibition of the Immorality Act were severely beaten and jailed.

Any music performed by persons of colour was banned, along with movies that featured persons of colour. The song "If I Were a Carpenter," sung by Bobby Darin, was banned because most men of colour were in the carpenter trade.

Publications of periodicals, films, books, and pamphlets were all censored, so it became difficult for South Africans to find out what the opposition movements were doing or thinking. Some people chose to become paid informants, spying on their neighbours.

Chapter Seven

Underground Activities

During this time, the African National Congress (ANC) actively ran illegal typing and accounting schools in basements or wherever they could rent space. Interested, I signed up for many of these courses, but they would only last for a short time until the police raided and destroyed everything in sight. Upon arrival, we found the government had boarded up these underground schools. Within a couple of months, we would get word that they re-opened someplace else, only to be shut down again. I soon lost my enthusiasm, and the loss of money paid, and I gave up the losing battle.

In 1957, at eighteen, my friend Patsy Janzen recommended that I apply for an upcoming cashier's vacancy at Wolfson's Furniture Store, where she worked. She said the cashier was on maternity leave in two months and was willing to train me for the position if her employer agreed.

Two days later, I quit my job at the clothing manufacturer. Summoning up the courage, I applied for the position at Wolfson's Furniture. During my interview, I told the manager that I had very little training from the schools that the government had shut down.

Mrs. Wolfson, a no-nonsense manager, took a chance and hired me. I received on-the-job training. I paid attention to every detail, taking notes of everything as if my life depended on it.

I worked as a cashier at Wolfson's Furniture Store for three years. Then, one day, Mrs. Wolfson called me into her office. My heart sank! I tried envisioning what I might have done wrong.

I entered the room. "Have a seat, Una," Mrs. Wolfson offered.

I sat on the edge of the chair. My hands felt clammy, and my heart was pounding. I made eye contact with her deep-set blue eyes, dreading what was to come.

"I like your chutzpah," she announced.

I did not know what she meant, so I remained silent.

Opportunity Knocked at My Door

She continued, "I would like to enroll you in an assistant manager training program at a Jewish community college in January. The company will be opening a new branch in the next year. I think, once you have certified, you would qualify for the job."

Speechless at the opportunity and responsibility, my tongue seemed stuck to my palate before I stuttered, "Thank you! I will try my best!"

Afraid of how my family would react, I never mentioned a word. There were times I came close to blurting it out but held back.

As January approached, I could no longer wait to tell my parents.

After dinner, while seated at the table, I told my parents and siblings, "Mrs. Wolfson, my boss, will be sending me to a Jewish College in January to attain the knowledge to become an assistant manager."

Silence descended. It felt like I had an out-of-body experience, hovering over my family as they sat around the table. Neville smiled and rolled his eyes toward the ceiling. The rest of my siblings leaned forward, elbows on the table, waiting for my parents' reaction.

My father took a deep breath, slowly rolling it out between his tongue and teeth, sounding out a long whistle. Mumsie removed herself from the table and poured herself a tall glass of water.

I was still hovering, and it felt like an eternity.

I heard my father say, "You are not Jewish! And who do you think is going to pay for your tuition?"

"The company offered to pay," I stammered.

My father replied, "We will see about that. I will visit your company to find out what's happening before you are arrested and locked up in prison. You know this is going against the law, he shouted, when will you stop being so rebellious?"

Pearl and Patsy commented, "Maybe she could pass herself off as a Jewish student?"

Everybody laughed as Neville said, "Shalom."

The following day, my father paid a visit to the company to find out about my enrolment in the Jewish College. As we sat in her office, Mrs. Wolfson calmed my father down by convincing him there were no strings attached. She thought I deserved a chance and was willing to pay for my tuition.

I attended classes at a Jewish College under the auspices of Mrs. Wolfson for the next twelve months. She also introduced me to finishing school, training in personality development, and cultural and social activities.

It was no walk in the park, trying to learn in a foreign environment. The students were familiar with each other, including the subjects at hand. At times, this new information and piles of homework boggled my mind. Each evening toward the end of the lessons, I primarily focused on getting out of class to avoid becoming too friendly with any students, especially avoiding questions about Judaism. I ran to the train station to board the last train home.

Attempted Robbery

Walking home from the train station, I crossed an open field about a mile from our house. One evening, I was attacked by a young Black male who tried grabbing my handbag. He started a tug-of-war as he tried prying it from me. Fortunately, a motorist's lights caught the action. He stopped, jumped out of his vehicle, and came to my rescue. The attacker took off and disappeared into the night.

The stranger yelled, "What the hell are you doing, walking across the field by yourself at this time of night? You are lucky he did not have a gun. Get in the car before both of us get killed!"

I got into his car. He asked me where I lived, and I felt his angst as he drove me home in silence. The stranger dropped me off at the gate of my home. As I got out of the car, I thanked him for rescuing me. Before I could ask him what his name was, he took off.

My knees shook as I opened the gate. I threw up, waited a while, composed myself, and waited again. As I opened the door to our home, my father said, "You are late."

Still nauseous and shaken up, I replied, "I'm tired, so I took my time walking home. I've got to pee," I added. I rushed to the bathroom and threw up. Afraid to mention my dilemma and the thought that I might be prevented from attending college, I remained silent.

The injustice in my country left an indelible impression on me. That escalated my disdain toward the government; for wheeling their power over another human life because they did not fit into the spectrum of their colour chart, preventing them from achieving their God-given right to learn and achieve their goals.

My parents and I will forever be grateful for Mrs. Wolfson's belief in me.

After graduation and promotion, I earned a decent wage, going straight into the family coffer. Mumsie provided me with a monthly stipend for clothing and toiletries as needed.

Chapter Seven

Pearl Converts to Islam

Pearl fell in love with Rashad Davis, a Muslim boy. The two of us kept this secret from our parents. Six months into their love affair, Rashad came to ask my parents for her hand in marriage.

There was no turning back; she was pregnant. My parents were livid! I was supposed to be her keeper during our outings and instruct her to stay with me. After my parents reluctantly consented to their marriage, Pearl converted to Islam.

She was now only to consume halal food. Adhering to Islamic law, all meat and poultry must be slaughtered by cutting through the jugular vein, artery, and windpipe. According to the Koran, animals must still be alive and healthy at slaughter. An Imam high priest must pray over blood drained from the carcass before consumption.

In the Muslim faith, pork is unclean and prohibited from consumption. Because we cooked pork in our pots, Pearl was forbidden to eat at home. My parents were visibly outraged at this arrangement.

Neville protested, saying, "She grew up eating pork." The rest of us remained silent during this new episode in our lives.

Pearl had to go through a ritual to convert to Islam. My parents refused to attend. As I recall, I was the only family member in attendance. Two senior Muslim ladies scrubbed her in the shower during the event to cleanse her from all impurities. After her cleansing, she had to repeat the Testimony of Faith (Shahada), "There is no God but God [Allah, i.e., there is none worthy of worship but Allah], and Muhammad is the Messenger of Allah."

After prayers, the Imam (spiritual leader) bestowed the name *Fauzia*. Henceforth, she was no longer known as Pearl. Fauzia staunchly adapted to her new way of life. Rashad was a good husband and provider. She bore eight children, six boys and two girls. They eventually established a custom upholstery furniture manufacturing company, which gainfully employed the whole family.

Aunt Sarah's Demise

A year later, Aunt Sarah died of cancer. I was grateful to have spent time with her during her illness. During our conversations, she asked me, "Do you know how you got your nickname, Sally, from me? When you were born, I wanted your parents to name you Sarah, but your father insisted that Una be on your birth certificate. That's why the family calls you Sally."

"Yes, I knew. Mumsie told me," I said. "Sometimes it gets confusing, especially amongst my school friends. They know me as Una. They think Patsy is Sally. Remember the day a boy knocked on the door and handed you a letter addressed to Sally? That letter was for Patsy. We figured it out and started to play games because we looked so alike to those who were unaware."

That was the first and last time Aunt Sarah and I had a person-to-person conversation without being combative. Although Aunt Sarah and I did not see eye-to-eye during my teen years, I missed her presence.

Under the Apartheid Law

In the Pass Law Act 1952, the government made it compulsory that all Black men and women aged sixteen and over carry passbooks within white areas. If they did not live in the area, they were arrested and imprisoned. This law made it difficult for these men/women to go to work or shop in the city. Black women who worked as domestic servants for white families were allowed to stay in makeshift shacks on the premises outside the family home and away from their husbands and children. These rules gave rise to massive stay-away-from-work strikes and protests.

Coloureds and Blacks had no voting rights. Many of us were outraged at these unfair laws. Neville, his friend Sullivan, and I attended many of these protests, carrying banners unbeknown to our parents. As a teenager, I loved the song "Shosholoza," meaning, "Moving fast, moving strong." Everybody sang while protesting. This song was also sung in tandem by Black miners and labourers before and during work each day.

In 1959, I, at age twenty, and Neville, age nineteen, attended the farewell party of Miriam Makeba—now-famous singer—and her partner Sonny Pillay, the ballad singer, at the Springbok Dance Hall in Vrededorp. Miriam Makeba first sang her song "Pata Pata," before leaving for the United States on a signed contract with Sony Records. The government banned them from re-entering South Africa for the next thirty-one years because the government saw their success as a threat and forbade their records.

Sharpeville Massacre, 1960

Ten days before my twenty-first birthday, Neville's colleague Sullivan wanted to test his new car. Accompanying him, we decided to drive to Sharpeville, south of Johannesburg, to witness and photograph what was to be a peaceful protest.

Unarmed Black demonstrators, including students, marched peacefully, intending to hand in their passbooks at the police station. Within minutes, the police opened fire with R5 rifles and rapid shots rang out in succession into the crowd. The police then baton-charged the peaceful protestors. Chaos and screaming erupted. People ran, and the injured fell with some trampled underfoot.

Neville said, "Let's get out of here—NOW!"

In fear of being killed, we ran toward Sullivan's car in shock. My knees felt weak. Some people were fleeing the scene, others running toward it. Luckily, Sullivan was familiar with the area. He turned the car down back alleys as fast as he could, the car's tires screeching as he knocked down a few garbage cans, as dogs barked and people ran. We heard sirens blaring in the distance. As we reached the main road, none of us said a word as we sped away in shock.

Sullivan dropped us off at home. "See you soon, buddy. You and your sister stay safe," he said.

Neville and I were unnerved as we entered the house, but we remained silent. The large picture of the eye of providence hanging on the living room wall seemed to follow me wherever I went that evening.

Later that night, the news reported that 69 people were gunned down and killed, and more than 180 were seriously injured. Neville and I looked at each other with terror in our eyes.

Lying in bed that night, I recalled when the first gunshots rang out. It seemed like everything was in slow motion as people were gunned down. The screaming and running broke the silence. Then the last word Neville yelled, with urgency, "NOW!" made us move out of harm's way.

The massacre sent shockwaves worldwide when the photographs of the dead and wounded were published. Tension ran high, and rioting occurred in many areas. The government declared a state of emergency.

This secret remained between Neville and me until years later. The horrific incident left an indelible imprint on all three of our psyches.

During a radio broadcast after the massacre, Prime Minister Verwoerd's said, "I want to remind honourable members that if the native inside South Africa today in any school in existence is being led to believe he will live his adult life under a policy of equal rights, he is making a big mistake."

Six months later, Neville and Sullivan got arrested and locked up in prison for three days for attempting to cross the border into Swaziland to attend an ANC rally. My parents were frantic, searching for a lawyer to get them released. Luckily, the lawyer got them released a day before their passports expired. This close encounter stopped them from attending any further rallies. Neville settled down and married Carol Ingles. They have three talented daughters. He is an ordained priest in the Anglican Church.

April 9, 1960

Two assassination attempts on Prime Minister Verwoerd occurred. He miraculously survived the two shootings by an English farmer, David Beresford Pratt. Shortly before his parole, Pratt died of asphyxiation, which was ruled a suicide. The police and security forces murdered many during the Apartheid era. Doubts remain.

Shortly after the Sharpeville Massacre, the ANC intensified their anti-pass campaign to gather mass input on freedom demands based on the "Principles of Human Rights and Non-Racialism," which resulted in the government banning the ANC. In response to the banning, they went underground. The government's reaction came swiftly. It charged the ANC, including Nelson Mandela, with treason. The trial was the most drawn-out in South African history, known as "The Rivonia Trial." Mandela declined to give evidence denying he was a communist. The trial concluded on June 11, 1964, resulting in Nelson Mandela and seven others being convicted and sentenced to life and imprisonment on Robben Island for the next twenty-seven years.

September 6, 1966

Dimitri Tsafendas, a parliamentary messenger, stabbed Prime Minister Verwoerd to death as he sat in his chair during a parliamentary session in the House of Assembly in Cape Town.

During these tumultuous years, many realized why the white-minority apartheid government put a yoke around the Black man's neck, keeping him uneducated and whipping him into submission. The Black man would do the dirty work, enabling the white man to prosper, preventing the non-white majority from taking over the government.

Chapter Eight

Fatal Attraction

At age seventeen, I met and fell in love with Vernon. He was tall, handsome, and had a distinct, proud gait that attracted many admirers. After a three-year friendship, he asked my parent's permission to court me, granting him the exclusive rights to take me to matinee movies on a Saturday or go dancing.

On Friday evenings, our friends gathered at our home to play board games, throw dart rings, or listen to the latest music under my father's watchful eye. Mumsie whipped up her famous pumpkin or banana fritters and, on occasion, my favourite coconut tarts.

Vernon and I got engaged on my twenty-first birthday. The family rules were staying celibate until marriage. Soon after our engagement, Vernon became very possessive, and there were heated arguments over sex. He tried to control whom I associated with, how I styled my hair, and what I wore. My father overheard some of these arguments and disapproved of his dominating ways, but I was in love.

Three weeks before my wedding, I overheard my father saying to my mother, "I disapprove of this wedding. He isn't a good match. Look at her—she's only twenty-one, a mere ninety-eight pounds, compared to him, a six-foot bully. I'm disappointed that she converted to Anglicanism to please him. I refuse to walk her down the aisle."

I stormed out of the bedroom. Sobbing, I addressed my parents, "I'm old enough to know whom I want to marry. With due respect, Dad, I will find somebody else if you refuse to walk me down the aisle."

Turning to Mumsie, I said, "I'm going to the dressmaker for a fitting. Hopefully, when I get back, we can continue this discussion."

The tension in the house was less static when I returned. My parents had decided it was my choice to make and said, "We are doing this out of concern."

My father continued, "I've seen how possessive Vernon has been."

Vernon's outbursts escalated. He took offence when I hugged a male friend when we met in a grocery store.

Vernon asked, "Who is this guy?"

Taken aback, I said, "This is my friend Trevor. He is the trumpet player in Elricas' Dance Band."

Vernon replied, "You hug everybody."

I assured myself it was just wedding nerves.

My wedding day arrived. My father was late. There were many arm twists to get him to the church. He reluctantly walked me down the aisle.

Controlling Behaviour

In the early stages of our marriage, Vernon kept mentioning, "My grandmother gave birth to fourteen children."

"I certainly don't want fourteen children," I replied. "I think it's too early in our marriage to start a family immediately. We have not discussed how many children we would like or can afford."

Agitated, he said, "I've waited long enough. I'm your husband and the boss. I noticed you have been taking birth control pills without my knowledge. This has to stop!"

Surprised at his sudden outburst, I replied, "Are you out of your mind? We have just started a new life together, and you are telling me you are the boss?!"

Towering over me, he said, "Yes! It says so in the scripture, Ephesians 5."

I was shocked at this early confrontation in our marriage, and the force of words and inflexibility scared me. I ran upstairs, saying, "Nowhere in the bible does it say you get to be my boss."

Vernon shouted, "Get down here! I'm talking to you!"

I composed myself and decided I would not allow him to bully me. Facing him, I said, "I don't like your tone of voice and the way you talk to me."

His eyes flashed. He slapped me across my face, pinned me down, and forced himself on me. I tried fighting him off, but I was no match. I had a flashback of being molested at eight years old.

I wondered if all men forced themselves on their wives. Repulsed, I sobbed in the shower. That night, my father's voice rang in my ears: "He's a bully."

The following night I read: **Submit yourselves; to your husbands**[7] (Ephesians 5:22-24, NIV).

I thought, *maybe it's my fault for not upholding my part in our marriage by not submitting myself to my husband.*

Moving Day

I had discontinued taking my oral contraceptives, and in the second trimester of my pregnancy, we were moving to a large colonial rental home in Doornfontein. Four different families were renting a shared kitchen. It was a dreary, wet day, groceries filled my arms, and I slipped and went down hard at the entrance, hurting my wrist as my groceries

7   http://www.christianity.com/bible/niv

scattered. I from the floor, gathered the groceries, went into the house, and wrapped my wrist in ice to lessen the pain.

After a few of Vernon's friends had placed the heavy furniture in place, my stomach started cramping. I had an urgency to go to the bathroom, and I started bleeding heavily. The men hurriedly drove us to the nearest hospital in their moving truck.

Upon examination, the doctor told us I had miscarried and needed a surgical procedure to clear my uterine lining. Both Vernon and I were inconsolable.

After being discharged from the hospital, nursing a sprained wrist and feeling sorry for our loss, blame surfaced, arguments erupted, and tensions ran high. I was unhappy living there; every time I entered the house, it reminded me of my fall.

We moved back to Coronationville and rented a room with Mrs. Barberis, an elderly widow. I was happy as we were close to both our families.

Unwelcomed Visitor

One day, preparing dinner, I opened the living room window to allow air to circulate throughout the home. Shortly after, when I returned to the kitchen, I heard a thump in the living room, thinking Mrs. Barberis had returned from the clinic. When I walked back in, I was shocked to see a young man, about nineteen years old, climb through the window. Through his bloodshot eyes, he looked just as surprised at seeing me.

Panicked and alone in the house, I took flight and ran to the neighbour next door. She looked at me and asked, "Are you all right?"

I stuttered out what had just transpired. "Oh my God!" she said, "It's Bertie, Mrs. Barberis's son. He was released from prison a week ago."

We ran to the nearest neighbour, who owned a telephone, but she was not home. Fortunately, my mother-in-law lived three blocks away, and she shared a party-line phone. Still shaken, I phoned the police.

Though I suppose it was not a matter of life and death, the officer replied, "It will take some time before we dispatch someone."

When Vernon got home from work, the police had still not arrived. They never came.

Bertie stole most of our possessions and emptied the pot of food I left on the stove. I tried pressing charges but was alerted to go it alone for fear of retaliation. Two months later, Bertie was arrested for armed robbery at a liquor store.

Living with the In-Laws

After this catastrophe, we moved in with my in-laws for three months. The house was small, six of us shared a two-bedroom home. There was no privacy and constant bickering.

At the behest of a family member, every Friday evening, we played dominos. The game went on until the early hours of Saturday morning. I was so tired on one such occasion that I drifted off to sleep, dominos in hand, and woke myself up with a loud snore.

I looked at Vernon and said, "I'm going to bed. I have to work in the morning."

As I got up to leave, a family member jumped up and turned the table over. Dominoes flew, and his whiskey spilled. A fight broke out, shoving and pushing as the others tried to calm the relative down.

I ran to my room and shut the door. After the fight settled and the friends left, Vernon came to bed. I said, "Why don't we move in with my parents for the next couple of weeks until the new apartment complex is ready?"

"We not going anywhere," he snapped.

Miscarriage

Shaken and exhausted, all I wanted to do was sleep for the remaining two hours before going to work. At 6 a.m., when I went into the bathroom to get ready, I was frightened—I had discharged blood clots. I woke Vernon, and we hurriedly walked across the road to the hospital. After examination, Vernon and I were in total shock when the doctor informed us that I had once again miscarried a six-week pregnancy and needed a surgical procedure to remove scar tissue from my uterus.

Still in shock the following week, we moved around the house like shadows on the wall, without saying a word to each other. I felt worthless, as I was not able to hold onto my pregnancies and ashamed of the stigma of not bearing a child in our three-year marriage.

I did not want to stay around the house and endure the silent looks or questions, so I returned to work on Monday.

A New Dwelling

We were excited when we finally moved into our newly built flat apartment, B. K. Reid Village on Fuel Road in Coronationville. These were the first flats constructed in the area.

There were five hundred of these flats, six flats to a row, all front-facing. A double clothesline attached to steel poles stretched out directly from one end to the other in front of each row. The homes encircling these flats were where our parents lived, where we grew up.

Accepting our loss, Vernon and I hoped that once we settled into our new flat and when I had gained some weight, I would be able to get pregnant again.

Home life was calm and peaceful. There were feelings of love for each other again as we dreamt of our future together. Seven months later, I was pregnant once again. On my doctor's advice, I took time away from work and carried my pregnancy to full-term.

In 1962, I began preparing for the birth of our child, and it was the happiest time of my life. I wanted to create a replica of baby Moses's basket in crib form. I obtained a giant breadbasket from a friend who owned a bakery and skillfully padded then lined the inside of the basket with satin material. I ruffled the outside with white organza and ribbon that covered the basket. A neighbour donated the stand. Blue and pink ribbons lay waiting.

We were over the moon. If the baby were a boy, we would name him Lance. Simone for a girl. The baby was due toward the end of September. In August, Johannesburg had its first snowfall in thirty years and was ill-equipped for snow. I had never seen snow before, and I was petrified of falling.

The Happiest Days of Our lives

On September 26, 1962, I gave birth to our son Lance, weighing in at six and a half pounds, at Baragwanath Airfield Military Hospital.

Conditions were crude; you were either wheeled or walked into an extensive delivery room lined with beds on both sides. There were no drapes for privacy, leaving all sides open. The midwife moved from bed to bed, checking on each patient.

As I lay on one of those beds, I heard women moan and scream in pain, scaring the wits out of me. I tried not looking left or right as babies were being born. Instead, I looked up at the ceiling and prayed for safe delivery.

Husbands and family members were not allowed in any maternity ward. These hospitals were for delivery; you could leave the very next day.

Mothers and their babies who were not privileged to have someone pick them up at the hospital were transported in old, rickety busses to the nearest drop-off destinations within a five-mile radius. I was lucky Vernon and his friend fetched me from the hospital.

We both felt such joy and relief bringing our son home after months of tragedy and loss. Vernon was proud to show his son to family, neighbours, and friends. You could not wipe the smiles of joy from our faces.

I was overwhelmed and sobbed as I placed Lance into his baby Moses basket and placed the blue bow at the end of it. I thanked God for giving me the gift of life and was grateful that Lance was healthy and that I survived.

I loved being a mother and watching Lance's expressions and habits change daily. Lance was content in his cocoon of blankets as he lay in his crib. I would check on him every fifteen minutes, ensuring he was breathing. As the months flew by, I noticed Lance's facial features began to resemble those of Vernon. Most of all, I dreamt of having a happy, stable family.

I was lucky to have Mumsie nearby, and she was able to come over to help bathe Lance, massage his little body, moisturize his skin with warm medicinal olive oil, and exercise his limbs, which was the custom.

This allowed me to prepare dinner, tidy the apartment, and wash the napkins. Diaper service was unheard of, so we used towelled napkins.

Unfortunately, two months after Lance's birth, I had to go back to work to help pay for expenses. A retired neighbour offered to take care of him while I worked.

Although I missed looking after Lance, it was nice to be back at Wolfson Furniture and catch up on the latest news.

Back in the Workforce

I bought a lovely sectional living room set and coffee table on a layaway plan to help furnish our sparsely furnished apartment.

After four months of being back at work, I felt joyful as I stood on the ramp of the loading zone, observing the men load the last furniture delivery of the day into the delivery van.

One of the men smoked a Rothman's cigarette and jokingly offered it to me.

I said, "I don't smoke, Basil. If I did, smoke would be billowing through my ears."

We laughed.

In a flash, I saw Vernon towering over Basil. I watched, in shock, as Vernon threw a punch at Basil, accusing him of having an affair with me.

A scuffle broke out, and luckily, one of the security guards came to the rescue.

The guard asked, "Who is this tough guy?"

Embarrassed, I replied, "My husband."

The guard stood astride, looked at Vernon, and said, "This is a place of work, sir, not a battlefield."

Vernon turned to me and said, "I'll see you at home."

My knees felt weak as the truck left.

Panicked and afraid to go home, I asked a colleague to drop me off at the nearest corner to my apartment. I picked Lance up from the baby-sitter, within walking distance to my parent's home—just four blocks away—and breathed in and out deeply, trying to calm down.

Masking the Truth

I opened the door and said, "Hi! Mumsie, I know this is short notice, but could Lance stay with you overnight? Vernon and I are going dancing."

Mumsie saw my angst and knew something was not right, but she agreed to have Lance stay overnight.

I kissed her cheek and said, "Thank you, Mumsie," and I left in a hurry.

I hesitated to open the apartment door. Rita, who lived in the same complex, leaned through her kitchen window that faced our door and said, "You just missed Vernon. He was looking for you, Una."

"Thank you, Rita," I replied.

I breathed a sigh of relief as I unlocked the door and stepped into the apartment. It seemed like Vernon left in a hurry; wet towels were on the bathroom floor, and dirty dishes were on the kitchen table.

I tidied up and waited for Vernon to return, but he never came home. I picked Lance up from Mumsie's the following morning. I was glad to learn from Patsy that Mumsie had a few errands to run that morning. At least I did not have to tell her another lie.

Vernon came home late Saturday evening. All smiles, he presented me with a bouquet of red roses.

He apologized, "I'm sorry for what happened at your workplace on Friday. I came to tell you that I would help Robert move to Roodepoort. Then I saw that guy flirting with you, and I lost it. Unfortunately, we were involved in an accident, so we decided to sleep over at his brother's place."

Livid and exhausted to argue and wake Lance, I said, "Thank you for the roses."

I ran upstairs, checked on Lance, and crawled into bed.

Vernon, Lance, and I attended mass at the Anglican church on Sunday morning. Still angry, I refused to partake in communion. Vernon glared at me on his way back from taking his. After mass, my mother-in-law invited us to lunch at her home.

I pretended to be happy during the conversation around the table. We talked about how proud we both were watching Lance grow over the past few months and how glad we were to have a place of our own.

We drove home in silence. As I put Lance to bed, unanswered questions remained in the back of my mind. Vernon avoided me by lying on the sectional, reading the newspaper. I ran myself a hot bath. Soaking in the bathtub, I was disheartened and in doubt. I asked myself, *Should I have accepted the roses and Vernon's explanation for not coming home on Friday?*

As I began to relax in the soothing hot tub, I reminisced about our first date, when Vernon and I went to a matinee show to see *Oklahoma's* musical. We were in love, and it was a beautiful day.

Our first dance as a couple was to the Cole Porter song, "Begin the Beguine." It was ethereal as we waltzed across the expanse of the dance floor. Vernon wore a silver-grey suit, looking dapper. I wore a pink chiffon halter-neck dress. We thought the world belonged to us as we danced the night away. That night, "Begin the Beguine" became our song.

Feeling emotional, I was glad Vernon did not come to bed before falling asleep.

On Monday at work, I did not want to discuss Vernon and Basil's brawl or what occurred after I got home. I avoided my co-workers.

Deceiver

When rumours circulated during my lunch break, I found out Vernon and his friend Robert were pounding the dance floor at the local night-club that Friday evening, accompanied by a woman named Joan and her sister.

I became curious and wanted to know more about Joan. I learned she lived in the suburbs and frequently hosted wild weekend parties.

As anger welled up in me, I felt a shift in my feelings toward our marriage. My first thoughts were of protecting Lance from harm, whatever the outcome might be in our marital life going forward. I had to arm myself against venereal disease and avoid another pregnancy.

Seething with anger and tired of all the bickering, I was repulsed knowing Vernon violated our marriage vows. I did not want him near me. I prepared dinner, trying not to mention a word of what I had learned during my lunch break. There was no conversation between us during dinner.

After Vernon excused himself from the table, I tucked Lance in for the night.

I bottled my anger for five days. The following Friday, I was ready to explode, and I went downstairs and confronted Vernon, asking, "Who the hell is Joan?!"

Surprised, he snapped his head back. "Joan who?" he asked.

"The girl you were doing the cha-cha with last Friday!" I exploded.

Vernon came toward me aggressively.

I said, "You are a bully, a liar, and an adulterer. If you strike me, it will end this marriage."

Vernon retreated, slamming the door on his way out of our apartment. I locked the door and crawled into bed. Sobbing, I asked myself, *How can two people, who were so in love three years ago, feel so much disdain toward each other?*

I did not hear Vernon come home. He slept on the couch that night.

Ashamed to tell my family about my predicament and hearing "I told you so," I remained silent.

A pattern evolved—an argument would develop on a Friday or Saturday evening, allowing Vernon to storm out and return the following day.

Everything went downhill from there. Unsure about our marriage, intimacy became a problem for me. The more I resisted, the more Vernon persisted. Forcibly having his way with me, I felt trapped, like being molested when I was eight. Both of us were unhappy.

I lost a lot of weight, which alarmed my family and friends. I told them that I just didn't have an appetite. Mumsie suggested she accompany me to see a doctor.

Vernon became overly demanding, forbidding me from visiting my family, declaring that he was my husband and would accompany me to the doctor if necessary.

By this time, everybody knew about our marital problems. It was not very comfortable boarding a bus to work. I avoided making eye contact with people or having any conversation with friends.

Not wanting to interfere directly, Mumsie asked Thelma, a close friend and neighbour, to keep an eye on our situation and to let her know if our arguments escalated into violence.

My feelings toward Vernon had taken a downward spiral. That night, I dreamt of standing on a poorly lit stage in my wedding gown. As I looked to my left, I saw my grandfather standing off to the side behind the curtain, crying. When I awoke, I had a foreboding feeling that I could not shake off.

Chapter Nine

The Other Woman

In June 1964, on a Saturday of a long weekend and after another heated argument, I listened to Vernon preen himself in the bathroom for his Saturday night rendezvous. It provoked me, and like a bolt of lightning, I removed Lance from his jolly jumper, grabbed two feeding bottles and a few napkins, and hurried to Thelma, frantically banging on her door.

Thelma opened the door and asked, "Are you all right? I can hear you and Vernon are fighting again," she said.

"I'm in a bit of a hurry. Could you do me a favour and take Lance to my mother? I'll explain later," I said.

Thelma was stunned, but Lance was in her arms before she could answer.

"Thank you, Thelma. I owe you," I said as I hurried away.

I slipped into the back of Vernon's Chevrolet parked on the road and huddled on the floor. Vernon got into the car and drove for what seemed like an eternity.

I could feel my heartbeat against my ribcage, and my throat felt parched. Sweat trickled down my brow as I prayed that Vernon wouldn't hear me.

The car stopped, Vernon honked the horn, and I heard a woman's laughter as she approached the vehicle. She got in and shut the door.

I jumped up from the back of the car and asked, "Where are we going?"

Both Vernon and his mistress reeled back their heads. Then, finally, she opened the door and ran.

Vernon got out of the car and dragged me out by my hair. I fought him like a wildcat.

I said, "Let go of my hair. You don't want me to cut my hair so you can drag me around, you coward."

Vernon pushed me against the side of the vehicle and asked, "Where the hell is Lance?"

"Why do you care?!" I yelled.

Battered

Vernon punched me, and I tasted the blood in my mouth.

"Get in the car!" he yelled.

Driving down a dark, narrow road, Vernon once again asked, "Where is Lance?"

I remained silent.

Vernon slowed down the car.

As the vehicle slowly passed a densely wooded area, I touched my lips and cheek. I felt the stinging pain and swelling. Suddenly, a vivid image of Vernon dragging me into the bush flashed in my mind.

Out of fear, I said, "Lance is with Mumsie."

By the time we reached our apartment, it was midnight.

I said, "It's late. We better leave Lance with Mumsie tonight."

Spent, I crawled into bed and thanked God that Lance was safe.

The following morning my head was pounding. I looked at myself in the bathroom mirror and was upset at my swollen lips and bruised cheek. As I splashed cold water on my face, Vernon rushed down the stairs, asking, "Where do you think you are going?"

I looked at him reflected in the mirror, and I felt utter wrath well up in me. My head felt as though construction drills were at work.

I heard Mumsie's voice whisper, "Count to ten before you react." I turned and threw up in the toilet while he framed the bathroom door, waiting for an answer. I rinsed my mouth and took a deep breath to bide my time until most of my anger subsided.

I slowly turned to face Vernon, and in a calm voice, I said, "Get out of my way. I have to fetch Lance from Mumsie."

Vernon still stood blocking the door, and with a smile on his face, said, "You're not going anywhere."

I brushed past Vernon, entered the kitchen, wrapped some ice in a cloth, and held it to my cheek as I laid down on the sectional.

"I'll fetch Lance from Mumsie," he said, locking the door behind him.

I got up and sucked on ice cubes, trying to cool my swollen lips. I sat in the kitchen, staring through the window, contemplating whether our marriage was worth saving.

The thought of Lance growing up in an unhappy home weighed heavily on my mind. I vowed I would not become the next homicide case. I wondered what the night held in store for me, and I braced myself when I heard the door open. Vernon entered the kitchen, as proud as a peacock, carrying Lance in his arms.

I was stunned when he said, "Let's go to the drive-in and watch *Peyton Place*. Mumsie already fed Lance."

Scrambling for words, I said, "It's past Lance's bedtime. He needs to bathe and go to bed. We can go to the drive-in tomorrow. It's a long weekend."

It surprised me when Vernon agreed and handed Lance to me.

"Your food is on the stove. I can't eat anything hot. After I tend to Lance, I'm going to bed," I said.

The next day, my lips were not as swollen. I tried covering the bruises on my cheek by applying a thick layer of pan stick makeup. I did not mention going to the drive-in, nor did Vernon.

Back at work after the long weekend, I felt embarrassed and self-conscious when my colleagues asked, "What happened to you?"

I lied and said, "I was in a car accident."

Mrs. Wolfson called me into her office. I burst into tears as I explained without detail that Vernon and I got into a fight over the weekend.

Mrs. Wolfson said, "You can't work with the public in your condition, Una. Take some time off and come back when you have healed."

I felt underwater as I thanked Mrs. Wolfson and left, avoiding eye contact with my co-workers. I boarded the bus and went straight to Mumsie's house. She was standing on a stool, reaching into the cupboard with her back turned as I entered through the back door.

"Hi, Mumsie," I said.

As Mumsie turned, facing me, I saw panic in her eyes as she observed my half-swollen lip and heavy makeup on my cheek.

"You're home early. What happened to you? Look at your face. I'm glad your father's not home. And where is Lance?" Mumsie asked.

"I just left work. Mrs. Wolfson suggested I take a couple of days off. Lance is with the babysitter. I'm divorcing Vernon," I calmly said.

Mumsie showed no emotion as she said, "I want you to think about your decision carefully. If you yell divorce out at Vernon, he might harm you. You should discuss your problems with your priest in a safe environment as soon as possible."

"Thank you for your advice and for listening, Mumsie. I will let you know what happens. Keep me in your prayers. I've got to fetch Lance."

I picked Lance up from the babysitter and hurried home. I prepared a steak and kidney pie—one of Vernon's favourite meals—hoping that I could suggest we seek advice from a priest about our marital problems.

Vernon came home from work and entered the kitchen with a sheepish grin, saying, "Something smells delicious."

Without eye contact, I said, "I got home early today. Mrs. Wolfson told me to take a few days off work after telling her we were involved in a car accident. So, I made your favourite pie."

After I washed and packed away the dishes, we had a cup of tea. Then, treading on eggshells, I said, "Vernon, our marriage is in trouble. I think we should schedule an appointment with the priest to get counselling."

Taken aback, Vernon angrily asked, "Who the hell have you been talking to?!"

Brazen Liar

Before I could answer, there was a loud knock on the door. Vernon got up and opened it to a pretty girl, who said, "Hi, Vernon, Kasim's car has a flat tire. He sent me to ask if you can help him."

I sensed Vernon was uncomfortable and did not invite the feline in. He turned to me and said, "I'll be back later."

As they hurriedly left, my intuition told me something stunk.

After he left, my legs seemed too heavy for me to move upstairs. Finally, I realized my decision to bring the marriage to an end was now or never.

My dilemma was approaching Vernon about his infidelity and lack of apathy and respect. And the reason for my disdain toward his sexual advances toward me.

A wave of sadness came over me as I thought about Lance's first birthday coming up in three months. I waited for Vernon to come home, wanting to continue our conversation, but later realized this was not the night to resolve the issue. I don't recall what time Vernon got home, nor did I care.

I deliberately stayed in bed the following day, hoping Vernon would leave by the time I went downstairs to feed Lance.

He was just finishing his breakfast as I entered the kitchen. "When are you going back to work?" he asked.

"I'm taking the rest of the week off, and today I have to take Lance to the clinic," I said.

"I don't want any of your family coming over here," he said.

I glared at him as he left.

As I was getting ready to leave, I noticed the bruise on my cheek was slowly fading.

Lance's weight and growth satisfied the doctor.

"How are you, Una? You have lost a lot of weight, and what happened to your cheek?" The doctor asked.

"We were in a car accident," I replied.

Doctor's Appointment

With a skeptical look, the doctor said, "I recommend you come in for a complete physical at the next appointment."

On Friday afternoon, I left Lance with Mumsie while I went to my doctor's appointment. During my consultation, I mentioned my head and earaches.

Examining my ears with an otoscope, the doctor said, "You have a ruptured eardrum that may heal on its own. If it does not get better in a couple of weeks, get back to me. And don't get any water in your ears."

The doctor suggested over-the-counter Grandpa Headache Powders to ease the pain. Next, he scheduled an appointment for blood tests at the lab, with a follow-up appointment as soon as the blood tests were received. He also booked an appointment with a nutritionist.

I left the doctor's office and did not fetch Lance from Mumsie. Then, enraged, I rushed home to confront Vernon about my ear injury.

I heard the red kettle whistling on the stove as the water boiled.

The Confrontation

"Where have you been?" Vernon asked.

Agitated, I said, "At the doctor's office. You busted my goddamn eardrum, you coward. I'm leaving before you kill me."

He stood up and left for the living room, grabbing the tall cut-glass vase we received as a wedding gift from the coffee table. He then walked back to the kitchen and smashed the vase in the sink.

I was terrified as he came toward me, pointing a jagged piece of glass toward my face, and said, "If I can't have you, no other man will."

I backed up against the stove. Then, in a split second, I reached for the kettle of boiling water and flung it at Vernon's feet. He jumped as the boiling water splattered against his leg, dropping the glass piece that exploded as it hit the cement floor.

Avoiding the shattered glass, I rushed past him and ran through the open door. Finally, I reached the clothesline in front of the door. He grabbed my hair, trying to drag me back into the apartment. I held onto the pole for dear life, screaming, "Help me, help! Somebody, please help me!"

Domestic Violence

As he ripped my blouse from my body, the neighbours peered through their windows; luckily, two big guys in the neighbourhood came to my rescue.

They punched Vernon and said, "Let go of her."

I broke free as they threw punches at each other.

Thelma, my next-door neighbour, stood at her door witnessing the altercation. When I broke free, she asked, "Where is Lance?"

"With Mumsie," I said as I tried covering myself.

Thelma handed me a sweater, "Don't go back into the apartment. I'll drive you to Mumsie's house. The guys will take care of Vernon."

We drove in silence. My only consolation was that Lance was safe.

Harry Jones, my parent's neighbour and the owner of a party line, had already relayed the ugly incident between Vernon and me to my parents.

I got out of the car, thanking Thelma for the ride and her sweater loan.

My parents and Harry stood waiting at the gate, startled at my torn blouse and the scratches on my neck. Then, furious, my father asked, "Where is that coward? He's lucky I don't own a car—I'd go to the apartment right now to straighten him out."

Expecting retaliation from Vernon, I said, "The neighbours took care of him. Let's get into the house before we have another public display."

I resolved not to cry. I was never going back to that apartment. Instead, I picked Lance up from the bed and hugged him tightly.

"It's getting late. Take a hot bath before dinner," Mumsie said.

My family and I ate dinner in silence as I fought back my emotions. I felt ashamed of burdening them with my problems after my father warned me not to marry Vernon.

I felt my father's frustration and avoided eye contact with him. I also had difficulty swallowing my food.

After dinner, while Patsy and I washed the dishes, I told her about the incident. She hugged me and said, "I'm glad your home, Sally."

My father came into the kitchen, "It's getting late; we're all exhausted. Mumsie has prepared the back room for you and Lance. Get some rest. We have a long day ahead of us tomorrow."

As I lay in bed, the day's events played back in my mind like an apparition moving in slow motion.

I got up and took a Grandpa Headache Powder with a hot glass of milk before I finally fell asleep.

Saturday at 6 a.m., a loud banging on the front door awoke the whole house. I jumped out of bed and peered through the window. It did not surprise me to see Vernon banging on the door and shouting, "Where are my wife and son?!"

Without opening the door, my father said, "Stop banging on my door. Come back at a decent hour, or I'll call the police."

Ignoring my father, Vernon kept banging on the door. The neighbours' dogs started barking. Mr. Jones heard all the banging and shouting and called the police. I opened the door when two officers arrived. Vernon stood behind them with a busted lip.

Trying to avoid an altercation between Vernon and my father, I stood outside and explained our situation to the officers. The officers noticed the scratches on my arms and neck.

"Is this a domestic violence report or a disturbance report?" the officers asked.

"A disturbance report," I said. I followed up by asking the officers if they would accompany me to my apartment to pack some clothes and food for my son.

Infuriated, Vernon shouted, "I want my son!"

One officer addressed Vernon and said, "Calm down, sir."

Accompanied by the officers, I packed as much as Lance needed. Vernon and the officers waited downstairs.

As I passed Vernon with my suitcases, I felt a strong sense of melancholy about what could have been.

I entered my parents' home, suitcases in hand, and saw the relief on their faces. After unpacking, Mumsie served us a delicious brunch. My parents and I discussed the ramifications of divorce, and they said the final decision was mine.

I thanked my parents for always being there when I needed them.

Spent, I picked up Lance and lay down on the bed, cradling him. I fell asleep.

A Woman Scorned

Three months after, and being back at work, rumours circulated about parties at the apartment every Friday evening that continued through to Saturday evening. All the "alley cats" knew what I had left behind in the closets when I had moved. And Vernon's girlfriend was pregnant.

Indignant at the thought of Vernon's friends sitting on furniture I was still paying for and no longer needed, it prompted me to repossess the sectional and coffee table at the apartment.

The following Saturday, while the party was in progress, Wolfson's Furniture truck rolled up to the apartment. Two big men served Vernon with repossession documents signed by me and removed the furniture from the apartment.

Livid, on Monday, Vernon verbally harassed me at my workplace during my lunch break.

"You've already started a new family; why don't we agree to a civil no-contest divorce and end this saga? I don't even like you anymore," I said.

The following year, at age twenty-five, I was a divorced mother.

Chapter Ten

Finding my Place

The Anglican church frowned upon divorce, so after my divorce, I left the church and rejoined the Methodist church.

Now living with my parents, I was determined to make a better life for Lance and myself. Reflecting on inequalities, I signed up for a few night courses, and I passed the colour-barrier test to find out I could not take part because I lived on the wrong side of the tracks.

I searched for a place to fit into and had time to reflect on the unfairness that domestic violence was not considered a crime. Domestic violence was seen as a way husbands could legitimately correct their wives. The thread of codependency ran through generations. Growing up in the community, I witnessed many mute stares from wives in unhappy marriages and wondered why they kept having babies. I was blessed to have had the foresight to leave the marriage, and I cringed when I thought I might have been further subject to harm.

I received invitations from three suitors during this time. One suitor said I was snobbish because I did not want to get involved in any entanglement early after my divorce. The other two suitors' parents disapproved of their sons getting involved with a divorced woman.

Nelly, a neighbourhood girl I had not seen in a while, hugged me and invited me to a party, saying, "Eish, Una, you are so darn skinny. You

look like Twiggy. Wear two skirts and put some stuffing in your bra."
We laughed.

At the party, everybody was downing whisky. Although I never partook in hard liquor before, I wanted to fit in with the crowd. I lifted the glass of whisky to my mouth, it smelt like boot polish. I mimicked my new friends as I gulped down the drink. It took my breath away, leaving me gasping for breath and neighing like a horse, which brought the house down with laughter.

Luckily, it was the weekend, and Lance was with his father. When I got home after the party, feeling nauseous, I lay down on the bed. The room started spinning, and not wanting to disturb my parents, I grabbed the gown from the hook on the back of the door and threw up into the gown.

Feeling shaky the following morning, I asked myself, "What's the fun of drinking when you feel so awful the next day?" I refrained from hard liquor and concluded that I did not fit in with the crowd. I soon discovered that the few friendships I had drifted away.

Loyalty

A week later, Kathy, a nurse and close friend of mine, confided in me that her husband, Abraham, was abusing her. She showed me the burn marks on her legs from Abraham's lit cigarettes.

Appalled, I said, "You have to leave this marriage, Kathy. I left, so can you."

Three months later, Kathy invited her in-laws and me for lunch. I was helping her wash the dishes after everybody had left.

Kathy said, "I have a secret I want to share with you, Una. For the sake of my children, I have decided to leave Abraham. I've shipped my personal belongings, and we are moving to a safe place. Please keep this between us," she said.

We hugged each other and cried. The next day, after Abraham left for work, Kathy left. Emotionally exhausted, I prayed for Kathy and her two children and cried myself to sleep. Kathy and I continued with our lives. We never saw each other again.

Police Informants

The tentacles of the Apartheid regime were now so ingrained that they reached into our private lives. There were people in the neighbourhood who became police informants. Tongues wagged, and party lines were ringing off the hook. Gossip spread about Margo, a girl in the neighbourhood. She had just given birth three days before, and someone gossiped that the child's father was Italian. Margo's sister took the child with her before the police arrested Margo for violating the Immorality Act and hauled her off to prison.

After her prison release, the police kept her home under surveillance. In defiance of the Immorality Act, two friends Wendy Marina and I visited Margo at her home. She told us about her humiliating experience; stripped naked, body-searched, hosed down, then forced to stand in the corridor to air dry before being held in prison. The police hunted down the father of her child, arrested and beat him, causing him to lose sight in one of his eyes.

Friends and Acquaintances

Word got to the police about our association with Margo. Wendy, Marina, I, and many others were now suspects. The police watched our every move. We collaborated, informing one another of any suspicious movement or gossip in and around the neighbourhood. I met many talented young men and women from families who afforded them the privilege to attend university overseas. Amongst them was Sandra, a well-travelled woman with a keen sense of style.

Sandra was engaged to Percy, a brilliant young man studying to be a doctor. Percy was fair-skinned and had beautiful blue eyes. Because

Percy's mother was Bantu, a Black woman, Percy was not allowed to share the lunchroom with his peers. The government afforded him the storeroom/lunchroom next to the toilet and stopped him from advancing to his full capability.

In 1965, Percy and Sandra had enough of the injustice and left for Swaziland, an independent country protected from the Apartheid laws. Percy worked in the hospital, determined to gain more knowledge. They later immigrated to New Zealand, where he became the first pediatrician to own private practice. They stayed in New Zealand for the rest of their lives.

At twenty-five years old, I needed to occupy myself on the weekends while Lance visited his father. Every Saturday, I volunteered to wash clients' hair at Vaughn's Salon, well-known for its fashion-forward styling expertise. The salon also did barbering. A month into volunteering at the salon, I greeted a handsome man at the reception desk named Juergen, a client and friend of Vaughn.

An Admirer

I overheard Juergen asking Vaughn in broken English, "Who is that girl with the long hair? I want to meet her."

Vaughn introduced us. "Una, this is Juergen, a friend of mine from Germany."

"Pleased to meet you," I said.

Later in the day, Vaughn said, "Una, Juergen would like to meet you for coffee and see a movie."

I replied, "Are you out of your mind, Vaughn?! Do you want me arrested?"

I told Mumsie about the German guy I met at Vaughn's Salon that afternoon, named Juergen, amongst other skilled tradesmen from Europe the government had recruited to work in South Africa. I also told her that he invited me out for a coffee and to see a movie.

"I wonder if the government authorities read the riot act about the Apartheid laws when they landed. I might have to take him up on his offer," I said.

Mumsie listened, then gave me the evil eye. "Don't play with fire. The police and the informers are already monitoring you."

"Yes, I'm aware. My friends, who live up the road, warned me of the little yellow Volkswagen parked on the corner watching all three of our homes. We also discovered the name of one of the informants," I said.

I realized the world was revolving around me while the government was patronizing me and many others. Wary of being under constant observation, Marina, Wendy, and I formed a coalition, and we decided we would give the police something to do. As soon as Wendy or Marina saw the Volkswagen, they would throw a stone on our aluminum roof, causing it to rattle as it rolled into the gutter—a sign for me to come out. We three would walk around the neighbourhood, not straying too far, and making sure we walked in well-lit areas. The police followed us for weeks without incident. Though our act soon ended, the police informers remained vigilant, smiling while collecting information.

First Date

My core belief was that not all men were mean-spirited. I swam against the tide and accepted the invitation to meet Juergen for coffee three weeks later. Wearing a pale pink blouse, a black pencil skirt, and black pump shoes with my hair styled in a French chignon by Vaughn, I nervously waited for Juergen to fetch me from Vaughn's Salon.

He rolled up in a 1958 grey Mercedes-Benz. Before I got into the car, Vaughn leaned out of the salon door and whispered, "Good luck to both of you. I hope you don't end up at Marshall Square police station or imprisoned."

We quickly sped away and enjoyed coffee and pastries at a secluded, upscale German coffee shop in Hillbrow, a vibrant cosmopolitan suburb of Johannesburg. It was the first time I had visited the area in my twenty-five years.

After coffee, in broken English, Juergen said, "Cinema, *ja?*"

Petrified, I asked, "Which cinema?"

"The Colosseum to watch *The Sound of Music*," he replied.

He looked suave in his dark suit while holding my hand as we walked across Commissioner Street, downtown Johannesburg, toward the Colosseum Theatre, which spanned an entire block.

I squeezed Juergen's hand tight with anxiousness. I was dazzled by the bright lights and the elegantly dressed crowd waiting outside the theatre. I looked around for any signs of police officers and was relieved when nobody approached us.

In the foyer, my head started to sweat. The combination of hairspray and sweat made my scalp itch. I could not reach between my hair and scalp to scratch the itch. I needed to use the ladies' room, so I excused myself. As I entered, I was astounded at the luxury of Dolly Varden dressers and velvet settees. I quickly entered the toilet, took a pen from my purse, stuck it in-between my chignon hairdo, and gave my head a good scratch. *What a relief.*

Once inside the theatre, comparing the humdrum of theatre design for the non-privileged to this, my eyes were agog at the vastness and artistry on the walls, depicting castles and the magic of a starry sky. I did not recall much of the movie that day. Leaving the theatre, I kept my eyes fixed on the floor.

Safely back in the car, I looked at the clock on the console and said, "Gosh, it's late. That was a long movie; can you drop me off at the bus stop, please?"

"No, I'll drive you home. Where do you live?"

"I live in Coronationville, with my parents and my three-year-old son," I replied. I scanned his face, waiting for his reaction. There was none.

Instead, he parked the car, took out a map from the glove compartment, turned on the light, and looked at the map.

"Ja, ja, I know this way," he excitedly said, pointing to the map. "I pass by this main road every day to my place of work."

"I live off the main road. I will direct you. And when we arrive at my parents' home, slow down and don't stop. I will get out of the car and leave the area quickly," I said.

"Can I meet you again?" Juergen asked. "Here is my phone number. Call me."

"Sorry, I don't call guys. I'll see you the next time you come to Vaughn's salon. I hope you realize you could be arrested, beaten, and locked up in prison for going on a date with me," I said.

I held onto my angst as Juergen slowed down the car. I got out and ran to the gate without looking back. I heard the car take off.

I quietly opened the door and tiptoed into the bedroom. Patsy and my cousin Pamela snuck into the bedroom, curious to know about my coffee and movie date.

Starry-eyed, I told them we went to see the movie *The Sound of Music* at the most beautiful theatre I'd ever seen. With childlike wonder, they tried to envision the picture I conveyed: the inside of the theatre, including the luxurious ladies' powder room and the plush velvet seating in the waiting room.

"Is he handsome?" they asked.

"Very handsome," I said.

After they returned to their bedroom, my heart ached with sadness at the thought that they might never experience the feeling and grandeur I had the privilege of seeing while Apartheid existed.

Chapter Eleven

Second Date

Three weeks later, Juergen and I met again. This time, he introduced me to his friends who had emigrated with him from Germany. I asked them, "Were you warned against associating with people of colour when you applied to work in South Africa?"

The only question the South African Embassy in Germany asked them was about Apartheid. At age twenty-two, these young men answered, "We know little about the system."

Some were evading conscription into the German Army and were happy to leave Germany. Once they had arrived in Johannesburg, the employment agency picked them up at the airport via bus. It transported them to a boarding house in Doornfontein, an inner-city suburb of Johannesburg, east of the city centre. They checked in with the agency in the following days, which then drove them to various companies that needed skilled tradespeople. Once both parties agreed on the wages and the skills that matched the employment posting, the company hired them.

When I met these young men, they were into their third year of employment and eager to explore unknown parts of the country, including those forbidden. They talked about the game reserves, wild animals, campfires, and a reticulated python measuring twenty feet long that were capable of crushing a human or a cow before swallowing them.

Intrigued, I said, "Wow! I would love to see a python."

I was chomping for them to learn about Real South Africa. About those Black workers who served tea on a tray at work each day who lived in shantytowns.

Some of these young men spoke English, while others were reading comic books to understand the English language. In South Africa, we talked in English and Afrikaans—a Dutch dialect. Afrikaans, Dutch, German, and Swedish languages are West Germanic languages. When listening to them speak, I heard similar guttural sounds.

I enrolled in a German-language conversation course at the Berlitz School of Language to appreciate my new friends. Still, I needed the correct address to register. Juergen accompanied me to the school, and we used his home address. For the following year, I attended night courses after work.

I drove my family crazy, sounding out guttural sounds aloud and greeting them each morning in both languages. "Good morning" in German: "Guten Morgen." In Afrikaans, "Goeie More." In addition, I practiced the language with my new friends, conversing at the end of the term. Everybody in my family was concerned that I was going to be detained.

I met sympathizers who disagreed with the Apartheid laws but were afraid to do anything. Some were afraid, some were indifferent, and others were misinformed. I encountered many poets who were unlawfully expressing their frustration through poetry.

I fell in love with poetry, and resonated with Vincenzo Galilei's famous quote, "It appears to me that they who rely simply on the weight of authority to prove any assertion, without searching out the arguments to support it, act absurdly. I wish to question freely and to answer freely without any sort of adulation. That well becomes any who are sincere in search for truth."[8]

Police Raid

While attending a multicultural poetry gathering, the police raided the building and loaded all of us into the back of the police van with no seats. They drove like maniacs on the way to the police station, laughing as we rolled around in the back of the truck. The police officers documented our addresses in a big book.

One officer named Andries started flirting with me. Smiling, he said, "I see you're already on file."

I remained silent.

Luckily, they did not mistreat us. We were let go with a warning. Once outside waiting for a bus, Marina, the poet, said, "I saw that young, Dutch police officer flirting with you. Una, maybe we should give you a Dutch name and call you 'Katrina.'" We all laughed as we boarded the bus home.

I felt guilty about not spending much time with my friends in Coronationville, so I made a date to catch up. I learned the police were standing on guard at nightclubs and social gatherings, ensuring that attendees did not violate the Immorality Act. The police harassed Britany, an acquaintance, for dating a French banker. The couple later left South Africa on an exit permit to France. I was afraid to divulge too much of what I was doing, as I would expose myself to danger.

After meeting Juergen and moving into a different crowd, my eyes were pried wide open. I visited the Kruger National Game Reserve for the first time in my country. I toured parks with sites that had built-in barbeques set amongst waterfalls and lakes. Large oak trees provided shade for the privileged, compared to Mia's Farm, where people of colour

8   QUOTES BY VINCENZO GALILEI | A-Z Quotes
    https://www.azquotes.com

were allowed to hold annual picnics, with its substantial red ants that invaded our picnic baskets. I recall a significant stream flowing along the flanked grey clay banks.

Occasionally, I met with groups of new immigrants who had no idea that the government divided the South African population into five main racial groups.

A Romantic Relationship

Juergen and I became an item. After spending the weekend together, we spontaneously decided that he meet Lance and the rest of my family. Upon entering the house, I thought, "Lord, if this is right, let me find a way."

"Hello, everybody. I have a surprise for you," I said.

Lance ran to me. "Mummy, Mummy!" My parents followed him.

My father said, "What sur—" and my parents looked at each other as my father questioningly raised his eyebrows.

I nervously introduced Juergen to my parents. "These are my parents, Mr. and Mrs. McCrae, and my son, Lance."

I followed by saying, "Mum and Dad, this is my friend Juergen from Germany."

"Pleased to meet you, Mr. and Mrs. McCrae."

"Nice meeting you, Juergen," my parents replied.

Juergen approached Lance and said, "Hello Lance, do you play soccer?"

Lance, fidgeting, questioningly looked up at me. I said, "Juergen's asking if you play soccer."

"Yes, I play soccer," Lance replied.

"Next time, I bring you a soccer ball, ja," Juergen said.

Lance smiled and said, "Thank you."

I glanced at the clock. "It's late. Juergen can't stay long," I said.

Juergen thanked my parents. "It was a pleasure to meet you," he said.

After Juergen left, Mumsie said, "That German man will take you to Germany and make you plant potatoes."

"No, he won't. All my new friends accept me for who I am, and Juergen accepts Lance," I said.

"I hope you know what you're getting yourself into," my father replied.

Excited, Lance asked, "Is your friend going to bring me a soccer ball, Mum?"

"That's what he said. Let's get you into the bathtub before I tuck you into bed. Did you have fun visiting with your dad and your baby brother this weekend?"

"Dad was crabby, and they were shouting," Lance replied despondently.

I thought *this did not sound good. I will have to approach Vernon about the incident.*

"I bought you two new fairy tale books, and you can choose which one I should read. Run! Let's see who gets to the bathroom first!" I challenged.

Later, I spoke with Vernon about the shouting during Lance's visit.

He apologized and said, "The baby was not well."

"Please, let me know ahead of time if there is a problem. I don't appreciate Lance listening to your arguments during his visits. That's not quality time," I complained.

Whoopee, we finally agreed on something.

I continued visiting Juergen every second weekend. He shared a large rental home in Parktown, a northern suburb of Johannesburg, with three of his friends. There were no home security systems during the '60s. For protection, they had four large German shepherds in their backyard. Each man owned an FN .38 semi-automatic pistol and a .22 long rifle. Every Saturday morning, the men and their girlfriends went to the old mine dumps in two 4x4 Land Rovers. The girls and I learned to target practice in the soft sand of the mine. The kickback from the rifle startled me after firing my first shot.

One of the German friends, Achim, often prepared a delicious German cuisine, *eisbein*, a pickled ham hock, cured and slightly boiled, served with cabbage, boiled potatoes, and a creamy cucumber salad. We girls took turns cooking when we were there on weekends. I gained a taste for dark German beer.

Police Enforcer

The following weekend, I sat in the park right across the road from my parents' house, watching Lance and his friends play. A police van drove up with two police officers. One got out of the truck, opened the gate, and walked to where I sat on the bench. I looked around, wondering what he was looking for; there were no other adults in the park.

Afraid, I called out to Lance, "Let's go, it's getting late." The children were having fun and paid no attention.

As the officer got closer, I recognized Andries, the Dutch police officer who had flirted with me two weeks before at the police station.

What the hell is he doing here? I asked myself.

Andries approached me and said, "Hello, Una."

Stunned, knowing I had done nothing wrong, I asked, "Why are you here?"

"Get in the van," he said. "I want to talk with you."

"Talk to me about what?!" I barked.

In a threatening tone, he said, "Get in the van."

"No! I'm not getting into your van; I'm taking my son, and we're going home."

By this time, a crowd had gathered around us in the park. I took Lance's hand, and we walked home. Andries and the other officer drove off, leaving the crowd wondering what had happened.

Shaken as I entered our house, Lance ran to my parents and shouted, "Mumsie, Mumsie, the police officer was talking with my mum in the park."

Both my parents asked, "What happened?"

I felt their apprehension. Not wanting to stress my parents, I said, "Just a routine check-up in the neighbourhood."

That evening, my instinct warned me something was amiss. The following day, I sent Juergen a message via a mutual friend asking him not to contact me for the next month; I would contact him. In the ensuing days, I spotted a police van encircling the immediate area around the park. Juergen and I had no contact for the following eight weeks.

Reconnection

When Juergen and I finally reconnected, it was my turn to prepare dinner. I made a mild chicken curry, served with Jasmine rice tinted with saffron, with garnishes of sliced oranges, mango chutney, and sliced bananas to lessen the picante. Most of the guests had never tasted curry and were looking forward to savouring the flavour. As we sat around the table, enjoying the meal, they were eager to learn what happened during my eight weeks away. They wanted to know my coping skills and how I could still believe there was a God amidst the unfairness of the Apartheid laws.

It was a highly complex question over a delicious dinner and dark beer.

My answer was simple. "I was born into a religious family and taught to believe in God and that God will help if we genuinely feel He will. My parents were people of faith and believed God would help even when things became uncontrollable. I witnessed people who claimed to be atheists call out to God when dying."

The Germans asked, "Don't you feel like fighting back?"

"No, I don't like violence. In jest, I added, "You can only kick a dog so many times before he bites you, no matter what colour he might be."

They pondered the answer, poured another round of beer, lifted their glasses, and said, "*Jawohl*." *Yes!*

Chapter Twelve

Vacation

We planned to go on vacation to Lorenzo Marques, the capital city of Mozambique, on the southeast coast of Africa. Its long Indian Ocean coastline was dotted with famous beaches and was ruled by the Portuguese. In those days, there was no visible Apartheid in Mozambique.

The vacation involved a lot of planning. The German men had to obtain a first-time visa entering Mozambique, plus re-entry visas coming back into South Africa. The rest of us needed passports. The approximate driving time would be eight hours, plus a two-hour lineup for border processing before crossing into Mozambique.

Our party comprised of four German men and four women: by nationality, two Afrikaners, Rhona and Hannetjie, then me and Theresa, who was Portuguese. She came from a wealthy family. Her father owned a shipyard in Lorenzo Marques, where we visited her. I recall being served tea in the most delicate eggshell, hand-painted teacups. I was afraid to hold onto the ear too tight, perchance it snapped off.

It took two months for the German men to get their visas. I had a problem getting a passport, as this was the first time I travelled out of South Africa. I was concerned Vernon would not permit Lance to leave the country at age three.

I insisted that my travelling companions continue their travel arrangements without me. If the government granted my passport, I would follow via plane, and Juergen could fetch me from the airport.

I received my passport a week later, but the law suspended Lance's documents. I left the matter of parental permission for Lance's passport alone, deciding to discuss this with Vernon later. I was grateful my parents could take care of Lance for a week.

I flew into Lourenco Marques on a one-way ticket. I was super excited and nervous, as this was my first flight. Upon arrival, Juergen fetched me from the airport. The humidity and temperature of 35°C hit me with a blast as I got out of the plane. Juergen had booked lovely accommodations on the beach. I needed to have a shower before touring the city.

Its people were hospitable, and the food was delicious. Mozambique relies heavily on seafood. Best of all were the peri-peri prawns, the lobsters, an incredible size, and the fresh fruit at breakfast each morning. It was relaxing to get away from the prying eyes of the Apartheid regime and feel the sea breeze against my skin.

Proposal

The Portuguese did not openly discriminate against its Indigenous population, who suffered state-sponsored discrimination and enormous social pressure. At ages nine and ten, young children lined up with buckets, offering to wash tourist cars for a pittance, to help their families. They were clean, polite, and shone like copper pennies in the African sun. We gave them something extra and wondered if they were doing the work on their own or if those in charge were taking the money they earned and giving them what they thought was necessary.

Juergen arranged a day trip to Paradise Island the following day. The boat ride was approximately one hour. Disembarking from the boat, we had to wade waist-deep in the ocean to reach the beautiful island— Juergen in his black shorts and white T-shirt, me in my one-piece palm-print swimsuit. Soaked from the waist down, we enjoyed a tasty lunch after we toured the white sandy beach and marvelled at the pristine turquoise ocean. Finally, we returned to the restaurant for a light refreshment while awaiting the boat to transport us back to Lorenzo Marques.

Juergen excused himself. Fifteen minutes later, he returned carrying three birds of paradise flowers. I thought it rather strange, as Juergen was a Virgo known for being more practical than romantic. He presented the flowers to me and opened a little black velvet jewellery box containing a diamond ring, asking me to marry him.

During our two-year "illegal" courtship, we had pipedreams about leaving the country someday and getting married. The thought of the seriousness of his proposal and its ramifications overwhelmed me. Unprepared, the only words that came out of my mouth were, "Are you sure about this? Don't forget my son comes with the package?"

"*Ich liebe dich*—I love you—we must find a safe place to live. That's why I explored our options here in Lorenzo Marques or Swaziland."

Elated, I accepted Juergen's proposal. He slipped the ring on my finger, and we kissed, held each other tight, and committed our love. We enjoyed the beginning of the next phase in our lives.

The boat arrived to take us back to the mainland. Our companions, who were in on the secret proposal, awaited our arrival on the beach. As we got off the ship, bottled champagne corks popped in jubilation, and the celebration continued into the night.

We had many things to discuss. We both knew of the many upheavals that lay ahead if we were to succeed. We explored Lorenzo Marques during the remaining days of our vacation.

We also celebrated Theresa's twenty-fourth birthday at her parents' home. They gifted her a brand new 1966 Mercedes-Benz 230 SL hardtop convertible. During our conversation, that evening, Theresa's mother suggested I accompany her daughter back to Johannesburg in her new car so that she wouldn't have to travel by herself.

The next day, we attended a bullfight in an arena. I marvelled at the skills of the handsome matador, and the picador mounted on a beautiful Arabian horse. I was happy to learn they would not kill the bull.

Our vacation was coming to an end. The decision was made that the women would travel in two separate cars. I would travel with Theresa. It was a long trek to the border, and we hoped to reach the gate by 7 a.m. before the busloads of migrants on their way to Johannesburg to seek employment arrived.

Waiting at the Border

It was a humid morning, and the lineups were miles long. The vendors with their boxes of sweet pineapples, bananas, and melons, with some already hard at work grilling corn on the cob by the side of the road, waiting for those getting hungry while they sat waiting. My stress levels mounted as we neared the entrance. Expecting the worse, I removed my engagement ring from my finger and asked Theresa to wear it until we were safe. She agreed.

My head was pounding; the smell of grilled corn made me feel nauseous. I step out of the car to take some Grandpa Headache Powder. No sooner had I swallowed it when it came back up, and I was too embarrassed to get back into the car. I sat under the palm tree in the shade and watched as the cars slowly inched forward.

As I waited, I had a panic attack. Was I capable of carrying through with the explanation about my return journey? What would happen to Lance? The cause and effect of my parents if I were locked up? What would their reaction be to my engagement with Juergen? My ninety-eight-pound frame began to shake as I silently wept.

Back Home

As I entered our home, Lance ran toward me, shouting, "Mummy, Mummy, I missed you." I gave him a big hug. His eyes lit up when I handed him the soccer ball and pump Juergen had promised him.

My parents were eager to hear about my first solo flight and vacation. I promised to tell them all about my trip after a hot bath. I put on my pyjamas and my hair was half-dried when there was a knock on the front door. I opened it and was surprised to see Vernon. Lance heard his father's voice and came running to the door with the soccer ball and said, "Daddy, Daddy, look what Mummy's friend bought me."

"That's nice, my boy."

He glared at me. "I will be late fetching Lance tomorrow. The baby is in hospital with jaundice."

"I'm sorry to hear that. We can exchange weekends if you like?"

We agreed on the exchange, and I was happy to have extra time with Lance.

My family was intrigued to hear about Paradise Island, the bullfight, and the delicious food. Everybody was astounded that Theresa's parents were wealthy enough to afford her such an expensive gift, and how lucky I was to be able to accompany her back home in such luxury.

Starry-eyed, Patsy asked, "Did you have the top down, and was your hair blowing in the wind?"

"No, we were afraid of being bitten by the Aedes mosquitoes that carry yellow fever," I said.

I smiled as I thought about the ill wind that blew through the building when the officers questioned Theresa and me.

It was getting late, and I was exhausted and bursting at the seams to tell my family about our engagement, but I was sworn to secrecy.

"Can I play soccer in the park tomorrow?" Lance asked.

"Yes, your dad won't fetch you tomorrow, so your cousins can visit, and you can have fun."

"I love you, Mummy."

"I love you more. Finish your Milo, brush your teeth, and get to bed."

Soon Lance was asleep. I took my engagement ring from the side pocket of my suitcase and placed it on my finger, admiring Juergen's choice of setting before I slipped under the crisp white sheets, hoping to get a good night's sleep.

I played back the scene, embarking on the boat and the proposal's surprise. The relief I felt at the sound of the rubber stamp as the official at the border stamped our documents, allowing us to re-enter South Africa. I was exhausted yet unable to fall asleep, tossing and turning as my anxiousness caused me to twitch.

Opening Pandora's Box

I pondered life before World War II in South Africa. There was considerable intermarriage between whites, lighter-skinned, and tanned coloureds who were absorbed into the community. That answered why some of my family members and others in the community were fair while some were tan and others were darker. Some had blue, green, or grey eyes. In contrast, Blacks had distinct facial features.

Through fear, greed, and wanting to gain white supremacy over the Black man, severe Apartheid laws subjected Blacks and people of colour to a rigid separation. Laws that prohibited intermarriage and sexual relations with other groups forced them to relocate to less than desirable areas.

Since meeting Juergen, we mingled with a melting pot of Greek, Portuguese, and Italians, some of whose skin tones resembled mine, and I was welcomed into their community. We enjoyed their cuisine, and I was amazed at the luxurious restaurants and the quantity of food and alcohol consumed—most of all, the constant wasted food while children in Soweto rummaged through garbage bins looking for scraps. I also met uneducated and poor whites working on the railway who the government had shunned. I learned that we are not genetically predisposed to prejudice; we're indoctrinated.

Being naïve, I was astounded to learn about inbreeding amongst different nationalities to keep their race pure or to keep their money in the family, resulting in intellectual disabilities in some or genetic disorders in others.

I felt robbed and angered, not just for myself but for those who came before me and for future generations who would be deprived of the joy of life's happiness. Young men and women who felt trapped in an unprivileged world, drinking themselves into oblivion.

Still awake at 2 a.m., I knew I could not go back to life as I had known it. I quietly got up and looked through the bedroom window, feeling a sense of melancholy as I watched the moon rise in the dark sky between the mulberry tree planted on the grounds of my childhood home. My eyelids were getting heavy. I got back into bed and prayed for hope before drifting off to sleep.

Chapter Thirteen

On Sunday at 6:30 a.m., Lance was wide awake. "What time are Charles and Brian coming, Mum, so we can play soccer in the park?"

"After church," I replied.

Mumsie was busy in the kitchen when I announced, "Patsy and I will prepare lunch today. It's early. Sunday service only starts at ten, so you have two hours to rest until then," I said.

"Thank you, I appreciate that. Did you have a good rest after your long trip home?" Mumsie inquired.

"A bit restless. Lance was up early and ready to play soccer," I chuckled.

Before Mumsie returned to her bedroom, she said, "I'll leave the two of you to decide what's for lunch today."

Patsy's Beau

Bright-eyed and bushy-tailed, Patsy entered the kitchen and nervously looked around, ensuring we were alone.

"I met a boy, and he wants to date me," she said, bubbling.

"Is he handsome? And what's his name?" I asked.

"Abie, he's boarding with Mrs. Arends opposite the church. He attended our choir practice and approached the youth leader about converting from Islam to Christianity."

"He wants to convert! That's unusual. Typically, Muslims expect the woman to convert. And Abie is not a Muslim name."

"Oh, Lord," I said to myself, "my poor parents," I recalled when Pearls' Muslim boyfriend asked for her hand in marriage and the discontent it caused my parents. Just then our father walked into the kitchen. "I heard my girls are preparing lunch today!"

We prepared *bobotie*, a simple traditional South African dish like shepherd's pie, with a twist of apple rings, dried apricots, and Mrs. Balls Chutney. Instead of a mashed potato topping, a mixture of beaten eggs, milk, and cream was poured on top and baked. It was served with rice and a green salad when the rest of our family arrived home from church, ready to be served.

We were encouraged to prepare extra food if somebody dropped by. We would have a potluck and a barbeque of spicy *boerewors*—like chorizo sausage—during large family gatherings.

My cousin Pamela dropped by, and the three of us continued talking about Patsy's new friend.

"He's handsome," Patsy said.

Pamela and I exclaimed, "Wow! Patsy, you have been holding out on us."

She blushed. "This is a secret between us!" she whispered.

"So, when are you going on your date?" we questioned.

"No date set," Patsy noted.

Pamela and Patsy were the same age. I asked, "Any admirers, Pamela?"

She smiled shyly. "Well, I saw this boy at church. His name is Kelvin, but I have not met him yet."

"Both of you celebrated your seventeenth birthdays a month apart from each other. Don't be in a hurry. We'll talk more later! Maybe I'll get to see these handsome guys at church. Let's make a large fruit salad and extra for three little soccer players and set the table before the troops get home from church."

Back at work on Monday, I was surprised to receive a visit from Vernon's wife during my lunch break.

"Hello, Una. I need some advice. Vernon's mother and I are not getting along. She adores you. Any tips?" she asked.

"Is your son still hospitalized, and how is he doing?" I responded.

"He's coming along," she said.

"I really don't want to get involved in your affairs," I stated. "You'll have to excuse me; I must get back to work."

One of my colleagues noticed Vernon's wife. "Trouble in paradise? I heard they have fierce battles. At times, furniture flies," she said.

"Really," I remarked. I tried avoiding any further gossip and hurried back to my desk, feeling concerned for Lance's safety during visitations with his father. I had enough to contend with.

On the bus back home, I felt a surge of joy combined with sadness. My engagement should be a celebration, not full of fear or shame. Dammit! I was more determined to find a way of getting out of this lifelong oppression by leaving the country and taking my son with me.

I was antsy for the next few days as I tried to cover up my anxiousness ahead of the weekend.

Mumsie, with her uncanny intuition, knew something was amiss.

"I noticed a change in you since coming back from your vacation. So, what is going on?" Mumsie questioned.

I told Mumsie about the visit from Vernon's wife and the gossip about furniture flying during their fights.

"He found his match. Glad you are not getting involved."

Announcing Our Engagement

I could no longer hide my secret from my parents.

"Where is Dad? Could the three of us please go into your bedroom? I have something important to tell you."

My father settled into his favourite chair, with Mumsie and me on the bed. I felt this heavy burden lifted as I said, "Dad and Mumsie, Juergen asked me to marry him while we were on vacation. I accepted his proposal. Juergen will come by on Friday to ask for your blessings and announce our engagement."

My parents glanced at each other, then sat silently, contemplating their replies. It felt like a lifetime while I waited, grinding my teeth in silent prayer, but I felt their pain. *Maybe I'm Wednesday's child*, I thought, *full of woe.*

Finally, in a severe tone, my father said, "Well, my girl, you are divorced and have a son. We can't dictate to you. Your mother and I never thought the friendship between you and Juergen was that serious. I'm glad you told us about the proposal before he arrived. Have the two of you considered the legal situation, and what would happen to Lance if you were arrested and jailed? There are many discussions to be had before the weekend. I advise you not to breathe a word about your engagement to anyone else, not even your sisters. We'll have the police banging down the door."

My father said a prayer for protection and guidance for the days ahead. Afterwards, I showed my parents my ring. They congratulated me and said it was lovely. When Mumsie and I were alone, she told me to keep my ring in a safe place.

Mumsie added, "This revelation was a lot for your father and me to absorb in one night. There are many unanswered questions. It's getting late. Let's get some rest."

I tucked Lance into bed and crawled under the sheets. Staring at the ceiling, I felt one load off my shoulders, but another added. How many secrets can one mind store? Would our plans to leave the country work out in the grand scheme? The one thing I knew was that I was no longer a naïve woman lacking in perspective. I now looked at life through a different lens.

Most people in our community had no cars, so there were no garages. To avoid parking his vehicle on the road, in full view of gossiping neighbours and police informers, Juergen arranged to have his friend Victor drop him off at my parent's house to announce our engagement.

He looked nervous. After cordial greetings, he sat and announced, "Mr. and Mrs. McCrae, I asked Una to marry me while we were on vacation, and I have come to ask for your blessings."

I shifted in my chair, avoiding eye contact with him.

"Una told us about your proposal and her acceptance. Her mother and I are concerned about your plans. As you are aware, you cannot legally get married in South Africa. Are you prepared to raise Lance? There are a lot of obstacles in your way, including Lance's father agreeing to him leaving the country," my father added.

"Yes, we continue having several discussions about what lay ahead. That's why we went down to Lourenco Marques, because they don't openly practice discrimination. I love your daughter, and I promise to take care of her and Lance wherever we decide to live. In a couple of months, we will further explore employment opportunities and living options in Lourenco Marques," Juergen replied.

There was a heavy silence, and the aroma of cinnamon and sugar on the banana fritters Mumsie had prepared wafted into the living room. "I'll make coffee," I said as I got up and checked on Lance, who was sound asleep. I felt the tension had lifted as I brought in a tray of banana cakes and coffee.

My father finished his coffee. "I have been watching your devotion toward each and wondered your long your relationship would last. I'll hold you to your promise, Juergen, and keep all three of you in my prayers," my father said.

"Thank you for being open and honest in sharing your plans with us, Juergen. Congratulations from both of us," Mumsie said as she offered Juergen another cup of coffee.

Juergen's face expressed relief.

"My friend will be fetching me soon. I thank you for your prayers and concern. Goodnight."

After Juergen had left, I looked at the clock and could not believe the discussion had gone on for two hours.

My father was silent. He rolled himself a cigarette and went to smoke on the back-*stoep* (terraced porch). Mumsie and I washed the dishes. "Has Juergen told his parents in Germany about your engagement?" Mumsie asked.

"Yes, he sent them a photograph of us on vacation."

"He sounds sincere. I hope all goes well. My advice is to be aware of your surroundings and keep your engagement a secret just between the three of us," Mumsie said.

After divulging my secret, life went back to as normal as can be. Patsy was auditioning for a part in a school concert, so the next morning, Patsy and Mumsie drank two raw eggs, supposedly to strengthen their vocal cords before singing. They were going to practice a few operatic notes to help Patsy. I thought, *Yuck, I'm glad I don't have to drink that.*

They had beautiful voices, but mine left something to be desired. We always sang while washing the dishes. After so much practice, Patsy landed the part she auditioned for.

My father smiled as he entered the kitchen while they belted out the high notes.

He poured himself a cup of coffee and returned to reading the early morning news written in Afrikaans and the *Sunday Times* in English. I joined him.

"Listen to this reading," my father said to me, referring to an article in the *Sunday Times*. "The government served many broadcast media and journalists with banning orders, making it impossible to continue doing their work. There are no signs of even a glimmer of hope. Although it breaks my heart, I don't blame you for wanting to leave this country for a better life. However, we will miss you and Lance terribly."

"Thank you, Dad. I love you."

Social Gathering

Vernon fetched Lance for the weekend. Juergen and the German boys had gone water skiing on the Vaal Dam, which allowed Mumsie, Patsy, and me an opportunity to visit with Maureen over tea and scones. I told her about my adventures in Lourenco Marques, omitting the proposal. We reminisced about our teenage years and shed tears for our beloved sister, Veronica. I was heartbroken not being able to share the news about my engagement, and the thought of moving to another country caused me great sadness.

Before drifting off to sleep that night, I fantasized about wearing an elegant pale pink full-length dress with a wreath of flowers in my hair on my wedding day, like the one I saw advertised in *Vanity Fair* magazine. I dreamt that I waited as Juergen rolled up in a black Mercedes, looking very handsome in a silver-grey suit. We wined and dined at a hotel I didn't recognize. After dinner, we took the elevator up to the top floor, where Juergen had reserved a luxurious suite. The elevator opened onto a balcony overlooking the vast expanse of city lights. He led me into the suite, where champagne was chilled in an ice bucket, and soft music floated across the room.

I trembled. My mind spun as Juergen gently undid the buttons of my dress and unrobed me. I laid down on red satin sheets. He slid between the sheets next to me and dimmed the lights. Just then, the push-button telephone at the bedside rang. Juergen picked up the phone and spoke to the desk clerk, and he hung up the phone, petrified. "We got to get out fast—the police are on their way." We hurriedly got dressed and left the hotel via the escape stairs, shoes in hand.

The Mercedes accelerated down the highway. Late in returning to his barracks, a young soldier riding his motorcycle sped down the road on the opposite side, trying to beat the deadline. The soldier veered off the road, hitting the dividing barrier, and headed toward our car. Juergen swerved the car, but it was too late. The soldier came flying through the vehicle's windshield. Glass shattered as his body continued exiting through the rear side window.

The car rolled over. I felt pieces of glass on my face as blood ran down my head. I looked over and saw Juergen slumped over the steering wheel. The sound of sirens and bright lights were flashing around us. Gasoline fumes filled my nostrils. I thrashed around, screaming.

Alarmed by the sound of screaming, my parents ran into the bedroom. Mumsie shook me, trying to wake me as I kicked, screamed, and rolled from side to side. Tears and sweat ran down my face as I sat upright in bed, feeling overwhelmed with relief when I realized I had a terrible nightmare. My father handed me an apple brandy hot toddy to calm my nerves. I was glad Lance was not home.

Chapter Fourteen

Cyclone in Xai-Xai

Six months later, Juergen and I flew back to Lourenco Marques, rented a car, and drove 217 kilometres northeast to Xai-Xai, to explore the area for possible employment. Halfway through our journey, we crossed a forested area of rough terrain with fallen trees, large potholes, overturned cars, and bits of clothing floating in red muddy pools. Pathways, roads, and safety routes were washed away, making it challenging to follow maps. We were fortunate to travel in a Land Rover and got back on track.

When we finally arrived at our destination, we found the beaches covered with seaweed. We learned a cyclone had hit Xai-Xai a week before our arrival. The tropical storm brought substantial amounts of rain over two days, and the water reached 1.4 metres above flood levels, breaking through riverbanks, which resulted in flash floods. Rivers of water and mud flowed down the streets, leaving many destitute, all while the temperature reached 33°C. Despite all this, we stayed.

While sitting on the beach, we befriended Jordie, a young Scotsman crazier than we were. He related his story. He applied for a South African work permit in Scotland to work in Johannesburg. At his place of employment, he met Jeff, a Canadian who also had access to a working visa. These two- free-spirited daredevils purchased a Land

Rover and attempted a treacherous journey across the African continent, intending to reach England eventually.

They were apprehended in the Democratic Republic of the Congo, beaten, robbed, and their vehicle and malaria tablets were confiscated. When they had nothing left to barter, barefooted, they were held captive. While there, they contracted malaria. Their captors finally contacted their respective consulates and released them into their custody after paying a fine. Lucky to be alive, Jeff flew back to Canada. Jordie remained in Africa.

Over a few beers, Juergen told Jordie about our plight. In turn, he told us about Canada. He then handed Juergen Jeff's address in Vancouver.

And said, "If you ever decide to immigrate to Canada, get in touch with Jeff and tell him I recommended you."

We thanked him for his kindness and kept the address for the next two years.

While in Xai-Xai, we learned about the communist and anti-colonial ideologies that had established many clandestine political movements supporting Mozambican independence. According to the guerilla statements, most Indigenous people suffered state-sponsored discrimination and enormous social pressure. These rumblings of discontent left us disillusioned. We drove back to Lourenco Marques and flew back to Johannesburg. Unfortunately, we lost touch with Jordie.

Swaziland

Still searching for a haven, we explored Swaziland, a small landlocked country in southern Africa, one of the smallest on the continent. The government was an absolute monarchy, ruled by a king who was allowed as many wives as he wanted. We abandoned our search and flew back to Johannesburg and had ourselves tested after discovering the Swazi population faced significant health issues. Tuberculosis was widespread. Thankfully, we tested negative.

Back home, the rumour spread that several people had been arrested and charged for breaking the provisions of the Immorality Act.

In the '60s, security branch members received special training in torture techniques. They developed a reputation for extreme vicious-ness and inhumanity in their interrogation methods.

We laid low for the next four weeks, avoiding confrontation with the law. At the same time, Juergen continued his search through various immigration methods, enabling us to leave the country. He found that Switzerland only allowed working permits. Going back to Germany meant Juergen would be conscripted into military service, which he avoided by seeking employment in South Africa. A Chinese friend found that Australia's Restrictive Immigration Policy excluded people of colour. The search continued.

That week, from the corner of my eye, I noticed the familiar police van patrolling our community. On one such occasion, there was a knock on the door. Lance was by my side as I opened it and was shocked to see Andries, the Dutch policeman.

I saw the strain on my father's face as he peered from the kitchen. Trying to avoid any confrontation between my father and the police-man, I said, "Dad, please take Lance," before I walked out and shut the door.

Standing on the stoep, I fumed. "What's the problem?" I asked.

"Is that your child?" Andries questioned.

Police Violation

"Yes, why do you ask?"

I recoiled as he smiled and lightly ran his finger across my cheek.

"Both my friend and I think you are pretty. Do you have a girlfriend? We could double-date," Andries hinted.

I was frozen by the audacity of Andries's request and that he thought he was entitled to violate my right by touching me. If I had no fear of being charged with assaulting a police officer, I would have slapped his face.

"Leave me alone," I fumed as I walked away and slammed the door shut.

Once inside, my parents asked, "What was that about?"

Not wanting to alarm them, I grumbled, "Just routine questions."

Without probing, I sensed my parents knew this was no routine check-up.

I had a hot bath and tried washing away that creepy-crawly feeling from my cheek.

That night, I tried reading the scriptures but could not concentrate. Tossing and turning in bed, I wondered what dark thoughts ran through Andries mind. And the irony of it was that the people in the regime and its followers were attempting to double-date persons of colour. *What's next?* I thought.

The Pencil Test

We were bombarded with negative news daily. Although disenfranchised, we laughed at the absurdity of the government's method in trying to distinguish race classification. The Population Registration Act required the reclassification of South Africans into racial groups based on characteristics. Since racial heritage was not always apparent, authorities concocted a variety of tests, including the "Pencil Test."

We read about a somewhat dark-skinned girl born to two white parents. At age eleven, she was subjected to the pencil test: they placed a pencil in her hair and asked her to shake her head. If the pencil fell out, she would be white. If the pencil remained, she would be classified as coloured. Unfortunately, she failed the test and was subsequently excluded from white school and reclassified as coloured. Her father passed a blood type paternity test, but the authorities refused to restore her white classification. The white society shunned her family.

Later, 518 coloured people were defined as white. Two whites were defined as Chinese. One white was classified Indigenous, another white became coloured, and eighty-nine coloureds became Black. This test remained until 1994 when Nelson Mandela became president and Apartheid ended.

Heart Transplant

In 1968, the following news overwhelmed me and many others.

The heart of Clive Haupt—who died of a brain hemorrhage—was transplanted into the body of fifty-eight-year-old Phillip Bleiberg, a white, retired dentist, which transcended the Apartheid law.

Dr. Christiaan Barnard, a young cardiac surgeon, performed the first successful human-to-human heart transplant of a coloured man to a white man at Groote Schuur University Hospital in Cape Town.

Questions arose about whether they exploited people of colour's organs to elevate the white privilege and if it would have applied in reverse.

Crime escalated in and around Johannesburg, I was apprehensive of Lance's future as well as my own in the years ahead. Vernon's wife gave birth to their second son, and their life became more quarrelsome. I toyed with the idea of asking Vernon for sole custody of Lance through a court order, allowing me to take him out of the country toward a better future.

It was the beginning of summer and a perfect evening. My father sat on the stoep, reading the newspaper and smoking his pipe. Mumsie was in the kitchen, scraping the pulp from a granadilla (passion fruit) to mix into an icing that would decorate the top of a freshly baked cake.

We had a sudden downpour of rain. Through the window, I watched little puffs of red soil rise as the rain hit the red earth and steam dissipated. I inhaled the sweet, earthy smell. My reverie tempted me to laugh and dance in the rain as my siblings, and I did when we were younger. At once, I felt a pang in my heart at the thought of leaving my homeland someday, but I was jolted from the thought when Patsy came home from choir practice.

"Hello, everybody, I would like you to go meet my new friend, Abie."

My father laid down the newspaper, looked up, and scratched his chin as he observed the trio: Patsy, Abie, and Pamela, who was looming behind, nervously smiling.

Introduction

"Dad, this is Abie, my friend and a new church member," Patsy announced.

My father replied, "Please to meet you, Abie."

I heard Lance in the kitchen ask, "Can I lick the dish, Mumsie?"

"Not before you wash your hands," Mumsie responded.

After Patsy introduced Abie, Mumsie remarked, "I haven't seen you before. Are you new to the area, Abie?"

"Yes, Mrs. McCrae, I'm boarding with Mrs. Arends," Abie replied.

"Welcome! You just in time to sample my new granadilla cake recipe," Mumsie added.

Patsy, Pam, and I exchanged glances.

My father excused himself to clean his pipe.

Mumsie hurried back to the kitchen to check on her new cake creation.

Patsy and Pam followed to make tea, leaving me alone with Abie.

Well-groomed, Abie wore a white button-down short-sleeved shirt with black herringbone trousers. His hair was sleeked back, ducktail styled. Sporting British black reading glasses, I got a whiff of English leather cologne.

He fidgeted in the chair and made small talk. "You and Patsy look alike," he said.

"So, they say," I chuckled.

During our conversation, I learned that Abie was enrolled in an accounting program at the same high school Patsy attended. My parents did not join us for tea, but we enjoyed Mumsie's delicious granadilla cake. After the usual niceties, Abie politely said goodbye to my parents and left.

After dinner, while busy in the kitchen, Patsy asked, "What do you think of Abie?"

The Inequalities of Life

"He's good-looking. Do you think he's sincere in converting to Christianity?" I questioned.

"Well, he's attending Bible studies."

Patsy and Abie got engaged six months after Abie's confirmation in the Methodist church. His parents disowned him when he converted to Christianity and disavowed the Muslim religion.

I pondered the inequalities of life: I grew up with a bias against those religions that forced their beliefs on others. Then there are those "two-faced" individuals who will socially accommodate anyone in the attempt to be popular.

Since rejoining the Methodist church, I had not attended for a while, not because some people whispered when I entered the church, but because I could not forgive the Apartheid regime and its believers who wallowed in the human cesspool. Those members revelled in the belief that they had the God-given right to deprive another human of their essential needs of life, leaving deep scars on their psyche.

"Don't stoop to their level, be humble," Mumsie always reminded us.

Many a time, I asked myself, "At what point does one stop being humble?"

I mulled over what my life would be like in a foreign country and how temperamentally different Juergen and I were: his passion for work and precision over people and my intensity about fairness, equality, and risk-taking. *Opposites attract.* There were moments these thoughts left me anxious, as I'm sure they left my parents.

A Close Encounter

Juergen fetched me from my parents' home a month later. I quickly got into the idling car and shut the door. Luckily, through the side-view mirror, he saw someone jump out from the bushes with a blade-like weapon in his hand. The attacker ran from the back of the car towards the driver's side. In a split second, Juergen accelerated the car and the attacker leapt forward.

We heard a thud as he embedded the blade into the right rear wing of the Mercedes.

The cars' wheels spun as we took off, leaving a cloud of dust behind us. I was glad he did not use his firearm against the offender. We checked the rear-view mirror to see if anybody was chasing after us. It was a relief when we reached the main road and saw the city lights.

On edge as we arrived at Juergen's home, we decided not to join our friends for our usual weekend of water skiing at the Vaal Dam. We kept a low profile, except for feeding the five German shepherds in the backyard. The firearm lay close at hand if we were to encounter unwanted visitors. We kept the car undercover in the garage. A week later, he had the vehicle assessed and learned that a bayonet/machete had caused the damage to the vehicle. We felt blessed that God had spared our lives.

Feeling like the walls were closing around us, we realized it was time to leave the country before either of us got killed. We decided to contact Jeff Laundy, the Canadian whose address we received from Jordie.

Immigration Enquiry

We wrote a lengthy letter to a total stranger, introducing ourselves and apologizing for the intrusion. We explained where and how we got his address and attached a photo of Jordie and Juergen on the beach in Xai-Xai. We reiterated the story Jordie told us about their attempted journey across the Democratic Republic of the Congo. We also explained why we were writing to him and requested any information that he could convey about immigration to Canada, employment opportunities, and accommodation.

After the weekend attack and the fear of police informants spotting the damaged car, we agreed that Juergen would drop me off at the nearest bus stop while it was still daylight. I took the bus home, trying not to feel self-conscious. My parents were surprised to see me home early. I was glad Lance had not yet returned from his visit with Vernon.

I said, "Mum and Dad, I have a serious matter to discuss with you before Lance arrives.

Juergen and I have started enquiring about immigration to Canada. I have decided to approach Vernon about legally gaining sole custody of Lance. If he agrees, I will forego child maintenance and grant him yearly visits with Lance. I would appreciate your advice and suggestions."

Because my father suffered from hypertension and Mumsie from angina, I chose not to tell them about the attack.

Saddened looks crossed my parent's faces upon my announcement. The ensuing guilt I felt involving them in my predicament and the flashback of the attack overtook me. I burst into tears. Mumsie comforted me, then left me with my father while she prepared some tea.

Heartbroken, my father sighed and said, "Well, my girl, we knew this day would come."

Mumsie returned with a steaming pot of tea and a plate of cookies. I could see she had been crying.

My parents asked, "Are you sure this is what you want?"

Pent up with emotion, I replied, "Yes, this is what I want. Lance and I will have a better chance in life. I only hope that Vernon will not fight me for sole custody. He has another family now, and not having to pay child maintenance would alleviate some of their arguments, whatever that may be."

"Knowing Vernon, prepare for a battle. It won't be easy. You better have a backup plan," my father replied.

Mumsie suggested we meet with Aunty Kitty, Mumsie's cousin who had travelled far and wide, for her experience and advice on travelling abroad. I felt the tension in the room subside as we agreed on setting up the meeting in the following weeks.

My father prayed for guidance. My parents hugged me and expressed, "We will always love you and Lance wherever you go. Have faith in God. Never forget your family and your humble beginnings."

There was a knock on the door—Vernon dropped Lance off. Lance ran into the kitchen, eager to tell us about his weekend visit with his father and younger stepbrothers and how proud he was of trying to teach the older brother to kick the soccer ball.

That night, I mulled over various ways of approaching Vernon on the matter of sole custody without confrontation. Should we meet privately or through a lawyer? What would his reaction be? Exhausted, I finally drifted off to sleep.

Devastating News

The following day at work, all the employees were informed that my boss and confidant, Mrs. Wolfson, had died of a heart attack over the weekend, and the funeral occurred twenty-four hours following the Tora. The business would be closed for seven days of mourning.

The announcement left me in a limbo of not being able to say goodbye or converse with her again. My father had met Mrs. Wolfson several times and was sorry to hear about her demise.

I was grateful to have time off with Lance and my parents. I offered to prepare supper. While I flipped through old cookbooks, looking for something different to prepare, Lance climbed onto the chair next to me and peered into the book.

He asked, "What are you reading, Mummy?"

"I'm looking for something nice to cook for supper this evening. Big boy, what would you like?" I chuckled.

"Stew with dumplings on top," he replied.

"Well, go and tell Mumsie what we're having for supper," I said.

He hugged me and said, "I love you, Mummy."

Patsy and Abie's Matrimony

After supper, Patsy and Abie announced they had set a wedding date in early spring the following year.

I was glad for the happy distraction, as I'm sure my parents were.

There was much excitement as wedding plans got underway. Although Patsy chose an elaborate wedding gown, they decided to have intimate wedding reception after the formal church ceremony.

After their honeymoon, they settled in a two-bedroom council house in Coronationville. A year later, Patsy and Abie welcomed their daughter, Kim, into the world.

Chapter Fifteen

We met with Aunt Kitty, who enlightened us about the *dos* and *don'ts* of travelling and living abroad, including the freezing conditions she experienced while visiting with her in-laws in Montreal.

She recommended that I leave Lance with my parents for a year while investigating living conditions in Vancouver after Juergen had sponsored me as his fiancée. Once we were married, I could send for Lance. My parents agreed. I was overwhelmed at the thought of leaving Lance behind.

Juergen received a letter from Jeff in North Vancouver early in the new year, acknowledging our request. He forwarded us the Immigration Regulations, Order –in Council PC 1967-1616, 1967, establishing new standards for assessing potential immigrants and assigning points in specific categories relating to their ability to settle in Canada successfully.[9] (See summary).

Jeff advised Juergen to contact the Canadian Embassy and request the necessary legal documentation.

Feeling optimistic while awaiting the application forms from the Canadian Embassy, Juergen applied for various advertised employment

9   Immigration Regulations, Order-in Council PC 1967-1616, 1967
     https://pier21.ca › research › immigration-history › immig...
     Authors: (Gagnon et al. 1967)

opportunities sent to him by Jeff in his field of expertise as a drafts-man/tool- and die-maker/machinist in and around Vancouver.

Within six months, Juergen received all the required application forms and methodically completed and posted them. However excited we were at the thought of Juergen's potential immigration to Canada, we tread water while waiting.

Prejudice Remarks

After Mrs. Wolfson died, a new manager, Mrs. Sorenson, took over at Wolfson Furniture. Mr. Wolfson introduced her to everyone. Once settled in our respective departments. I politely introduced myself, as we would be sharing the same space,

"Welcome, Mrs. Sorenson. My name is Una."

Mrs. Sorenson looked at me and said, "So you are the little brown girl I heard Mrs. Wolfson was so fond of."

Immediately, a red flag went up for her racist remark, leaving a bitter taste in my mouth. I said to myself, Count to ten before you say anything. The late Mrs. Wolfson's face flashed before me.

I stood tall and countered, "Yes, Mrs. Wolfson and I respected each other. I will miss her."

The new manager glared at me. I excused myself from her office.

In the following months, Mrs. Sorenson caught wind of my involvement with Juergen. Soon after, she said, "That's a lovely dress you're wearing, Una. Did your German boyfriend buy it for you?" She snickered.

I stopped in my tracks but refused to let her get the better of me or stoop to her level.

I said, "Lovely, isn't it?"

Knowing our working relationship would go nowhere and there was no workers' union to protect me against prejudice, I refused to work with a provoking bigot. After ten years of gainful employment, I quit my job at Wolfson's Furniture.

An Analogy of Prejudice

Prejudice is akin to a parent or a friend teaching

A child how to skim pebbles across the water.

Enjoying the effect as the ripples grow wider.

Eventually, the pebbles and the ripples are swept up by incoming waves.

Carried across the ocean far and wide . . .

Battered by enormous currents.

Bashed against rocks, tumbled in white caps.

Some pebbles survive tsunamis. Others are pulverized into powdered sand, washed up onto a

Beach in some foreign land.

If someday a prejudice thorn influences a decision you make solely or collectively on another.

Human life, leave that closed mind ajar.

Reflect upon the rippling cause and effect on that human's journey in the circle of life.

If you were in their shoes, would you survive?

Making Amends

I received a good severance package from Wolfson's Furniture Company. Although I missed my long-time colleagues, I was glad to spend the following two months with my parents and Lance. During conversations with my parents, we reminisced about my teenage years and all the beautiful times our family shared, including the hard times.

My father apologized for all the hidings he gave me during my teenage years.

"There were so many young girls who were promiscuous in the neighbourhood, resulting in unwanted pregnancies," he said. "And knowing how strong-willed you are, I thought the leather strap would prevent you from going astray. I did it for your sake."

At age twenty-nine, I was bold enough to tell my parents, "You need not have worried about me. I was so naïve and afraid of shaming you by having sex before marriage. Sex was one of the reasons Vernon and I did not see eye to eye, which caused many of our arguments before we wed. I wished your generation could educate us about sex at an early age."

I felt a sense of unease as Mumsie shifted in her chair. Not wanting to make my parents feel guilty, I said, "I love and appreciate the sacrifices you made to ensure the well-being of our family. Thank you for your patience in overcoming my stubbornness and teaching me that life is all about choices and the consequences of making the wrong choice. You strapped me for disobedience. You never gave up on me."

A weight lifted off my shoulders as we hugged and forgave each other.

We bought flowers and visited the graveside of my departed sister, Veronica. I revealed to my parents, "I felt sad when Veronica got engaged at age eighteen, albeit she was two years older than me. She never disobeyed you. I wished she had joined me in experiencing the rhythm of music and the cadence of the tango and shared my heartbreak when I broke up with my boyfriend before she got married to a man ten years her senior. It broke my heart when her life was suddenly cut short. I hoped she was happy."

We said a prayer and left.

Preparing Lance for Future Flights

During my time off, Mumsie and I had long conversations while preparing meals or trying new baking recipes in the kitchen. We shed many tears about my possible imminent departure to Canada. Although our discussions were pensive, we mused about what living in another country would be like: what clothing did Canadians wear to keep warm? Would I adapt to the freezing temperature and being away from the family?

The thought of what Vernon and I would do to prepare Lance for the possibility of me leaving him in the care of my parents while I was in Canada was heartbreaking. I wondered what Lance's response would be, and it left me in an emotional tailspin.

I watched Lance and his cousins play war games in the backyard, donning their helmets and impersonating soldiers while shooting the enemy with their toy guns. There was much warlike activity as they shouted, "The Germans are coming, the Germans are coming!" Such a ruckus caused the neighbour's dogs to bark with excitement. Two soldiers fell in battle while trying to quiet the dogs. One of the younger soldiers lost his helmet while jumping over their bodies. The older cousins threw paper airplanes in the air. One aircraft flew over the fence and went down in the churchyard. Luckily, there were no injuries.

The war abruptly ended when we called them into the mess hall. These soldiers cleaned up before we served them hot chocolate and biscuits. It made me smile at their childhood innocence. I wondered what Juergen would think about these war games.

I gently coaxed Lance by asking, "Would you like to fly in an airplane?"

Lance looked at me wide-eyed, thought about it, then asked, "Won't it crash?"

"No, it won't crash. Remember when I went on an airplane and flew to Lourenco Marques? I came home safely. Next week, I will take you to the airport, and we can watch the big planes take off."

"Are we going on the plane?"

"No, we're going to watch them take off," I replied.

Excited, he asked, "Are Mumsie and Pop [my dad] going with us?"

"Of course," my father replied.

The following Friday morning, we boarded a bus to the international airport. We sat in the waiting area close to a large window. In anticipation, Lance pressed his face against the windowpane as we watched the planes lift off and disappear into the horizon.

That night, Lance kept pestering me, "When are we going on a plane? Can you touch the clouds? Do you have money for the tickets, Mummy?"

"Not yet," I replied. "I must save a lot of money. Now, let's get ready for bed. We must get up early; we're going to the big market with Pop in the morning."

New Employment

Two months later, Gloria Meyer, a close friend, informed me about a switchboard operator's position opening at S. A. Bias Binding Company where she was employed. I jumped at the opportunity. The following week, I received on-the-job training on a plug-in manual switchboard. I held this position until I emigrated from South Africa.

S. A. Bias Binding was a large Jewish-owned manufacturing company of lace, bias binding, and trimmings. The owner, Mr. Sam Clapper, was fair and unbiased. Gloria and I were the only non-Jewish employees in the office. Although my new job differed from what I was doing at Wolfson's Furniture, I enjoyed being away from the discord. Mrs. Helps, a stern woman in charge of shipping, randomly searched Black factory workers before they left for the day, making sure they had no lace wrapped around their bodies.

Gloria and I travelled for forty-five minutes to Jeppe Street Station. The commute gave us time to knit a few more rows on the fair-isle sweater patterns we were knitting for our young sons. Hers had colourful balloons on the back of the sweater. Mine was a horse. It was a challenge for both of us as we concentrated on intertwining the different colours of wool into the patterns while not missing our train stop.

Chapter Sixteen

Telephone Harassment

T he police tried tripping me up with questions on the party line at home.

"Hi Una, this is Pete. I believe you know Juergen, a friend of mine. Do you have his telephone number?" he asked.

A red flag immediately flashed in my mind. I thought, "Hmm, it's your friend. Why don't you have his number? And where did you get mine?"

Before answering, I was appalled when I realized the neighbour had been eavesdropping in our conversation when I heard an "Shh."

"I'm sorry, you have the wrong number," I replied and slammed the phone.

A few days later, while I was at work, Mumsie received an annoying phone call from someone looking for Juergen, who inquired if Lance was Juergen's son. The caller implied that I might have breached the Immorality Act.

Our Beloved Fathers Demise

On August 13, 1968, my father suffered a massive stroke and passed on, leaving an empty crater in our lives that were hard to accept. It seemed like my lifeboat was wrenched from its mooring place as I struggled to stay afloat. At the same time, my siblings and I moved around in a trance. Mumsie got down to business and gathered us around her.

She said, "Your dad has left this world for a better place. Let's honour him by lifting our heads high and moving in unison as we lay him to rest."

We arranged church and funeral services. As was the custom, we served tea as neighbours and friends came to sympathize, offering their assistance. Some offered to make wreaths. Others took over arranging two double-decker busses to transport attendees to the cemetery, as very few had vehicles. The pastor's wife booked the church basement and assigned members to prepare a potluck lunch after the service. We laughed and cried together.

Once everybody had left, we felt that pang of emptiness that once filled the space with love and hope. We mourned our father by wearing black clothing for the following three months.

I felt resentful that he lived through an age of anxiety for sixty-one years, through no fault of his own. Did he feel annihilated when the Apartheid government trashed 80.7 percent of the population in 1949 with one pen stroke? What were his thoughts when his father abandoned his mother?

Driving to the graveyard on the morning of my father's funeral, my eyelids were swollen from weeping. I watched the procession that followed, recalling all those precious moments we shared. Standing at the graveside, I saw Vernon standing on a mound of red soil overlooking the grave. Juergen attended the church service, not wanting to look conspicuous in a crowd at the cemetery.

"Goodbye, Dad," I said. "You worked your fingers to the bone to make our lives better. I will make you proud."

Exhausted after the grieving and activity, we were thankful to be left alone as a family. Mumsie had a hot bath and retired to the quiet of her bedroom. My siblings and I had a hot cup of tea and reminisced through our tears. We checked on Mumsie occasionally, making sure she did not need anything. It was comforting to have the whole family sleeping under one roof.

That night in bed, Lance crawled up next to me and said, "Shame that Pop is in that big hole by himself. He's going to get cold. Does he have a blanket? Is he going to live in the hole, Mummy?"

"He has a nice, warm suit jacket on, and no, he's not going to live in the hole. He's already in heaven," I said.

"Can he visit us? Who will take me to school when I'm old enough?"

"No, he can't visit us, but he will always love us. Your dad will take you to school on the first day. After that, you can walk to school with your cousins. Are you excited to start school soon?"

"Yes, but I will miss Pop," he said before he dropped off to sleep.

The following morning, Lance got up early and went to Mumsie's bedroom to check if my father was in his bedroom. Then for a while, Lance was clingy. I was glad to have him visit Vernon as a diversion.

A week later, before visiting the grave, we entered a small, dingy office. A clerk flipped through a large book whose pages had turned yellow with age to find the plot number. Our father's plot was not far from Veronica's grave.

My father's grave had a mound of red soil along its length. Most could not afford a gravestone; instead, bronzed spikes with plot numbers were embedded in the ground at the foot of the graves for identification. We removed the dried wreaths, sprinkled water on both graves, and filled the vases with fresh flowers. After saying prayers, we walked back home in heavy-laden mud-splattered shoes along the two-mile well-trodden path. I felt weary.

Sitting at the dinner table, I could not fathom that my father would never again walk through the door and join us at the head of the table. Our conversations focused on memories as we realized life as we knew it had changed forever.

We were fortunate to have close family connections, caring friends, and neighbours who helped us accept and heal through bits and pieces. Although the pain slowly eased, the memories remain forever. Mumsie was the glue that kept the family together for generations.

Jubilation and Sorrow Mingled

The week following my father's burial, Juergen received his Permanent Resident Immigration Visa to Canada with a six-month expiry date of March the following year. He had to complete his final paperwork, including filing his tax returns and selling his vehicle and household belongings.

He received a welcoming letter from Jeff, offering him homestay accommodation at his parents' home in Lynn Valley, North Vancouver, upon his arrival.

We greeted the news with much jubilation and anticipation, looking forward to new beginnings. However, I felt saddened that Juergen would soon be leaving Johannesburg without us. I didn't know when I'd see him again.

Daunting News

My worst fears surfaced the following week when I received the daunting news from my lawyer, leaving us in a tailspin. Vernon and I had agreed on sole custody with a proposal for visitation rights if I were to leave the country. He reneged on signing the legal documents for Lance's passport, delaying the process for two years.

Falling short of confronting Vernon, we painted our family home to work out my frustrations and to prepare our home before Christmas. I recalled my father obtaining four gallons of smelly grey oil-based paint from the city council in October; he painted the walls every three years. The stinky smell always prompted me to try weaselling out of being around to help, so we left the doors and windows open for days to eliminate the smell. Luckily, it was spring, and Johannesburg's temperature rose to 20°C.

As we busied ourselves with painting the walls, the aroma of sweet pink honeysuckle vines, symbolizing love lost, permeated the air. I visualized my father looking down on us from heaven, saying, "Well done, girls."

All other Christmas preparations continued—knitting projects to complete for gift-giving and sending out Christmas cards. We made crepe paper streamers and bells as Christmas decorations.

Munsie kept busy baking tarts and steaming Christmas puddings to sell. Then, sorting my father's clothes for donation and wrote thank you notes to those who helped during our grief. As temperatures climbed above twenty degrees, we shed our mourning clothes. I felt lighter.

I had doubts about Lance and me joining Juergen in Vancouver in the foreseeable future. Each night as I lay awake in bed during the early morning hours, a little voice in my head kept saying, "Have faith."

Desperate, I visited a well-known fortune teller in the neighbourhood who read tea leaves. After I drank my tea, she turned the cup upside down in the saucer and shut her eyes for a few minutes while I waited.

She opened her eyes, turned the cup back up, stared into the cup, and said, "I see a large body of water. Are you planning a holiday?"

"No," I replied.

She peered back into the cup. "I see a quick exit, mountains, and a well-organized man in your future."

Leary of revealing any information, I did not ask any questions. I paid her the allotted fee and hurried home.

On Christmas Eve, my siblings gathered at our house to exchange homemade gifts and listen to Christmas music over the radio. We helped Mumsie prepare the steak and kidney pies, and we strained and bottled the ginger beer.

Juergen joined us for lunch after early morning mass on Christmas Day. Although it was summer, Juergen introduced the adults to hot mulled wine that consisted of merlot, brandy, oranges, and whole spices of cinnamon, star anise, cloves, and a bit of honey. The children enjoyed the ginger beer. After, Juergen's friend fetched him, and when the children were safely in bed, we adults indulged in the mulled wine and raised our mugs, wishing my father and Veronica a Merry Christmas. After a few drinks, we felt mellow.

Questions and Answers

On New Year's Eve, we attended midnight mass. As the new year rolled in, people revelled in banging pots and pans and setting off fireworks. Those who participated in the midnight ball were back on the bus at 7 a.m. to prepare for the picnic at Mia's Farm. For the first time, our family did not participate in the annual revelry. After our family barbecue, the adults gathered in the living room. Mumsie sat quietly in a comfortable chair. Curious, Maureen asked me, "When will Juergen be leaving?"

"At the end of January. He will fly back to Germany to visit his parents before continuing to Canada," I added.

"What will you do if he doesn't send for you?" Patsy inquired.

"I trust he will. If not, I will take Lance and leave this unfair, godforsaken country, where if you dare stand up for yourself, the government beat you into submission," I cursed.

"Don't forget about us wherever you go," replied Pam.

"Oh, by the way," I said, "I went to the fortune-teller, and she saw a large body of water and a man who pays careful attention to details in my future. And a quick exit."

Neville chimed in, "Indeed, Juergen's making a quick exit."

Looking weary, Mumsie got up from her chair and announced, "It's getting late. Let's bow our heads and pray for guidance and protection in the new year."

"I would like to visit the fortune teller with you. Let's set a date," Maureen said before leaving.

Mumsie gave us the evil eye.

Point of Departure

As Juergen's departure loomed, I asked, "Are you sure you're ready for marriage and the responsibility of raising a child? Now is the time to let me know if you had a change of heart."

Juergen looked at me and said, "You're the love of my life. Don't doubt me now after everything we've gone through these past five years. I promise, as soon as I find gainful employment in Vancouver and feel settled, I will send for you and Lance."

Ecstatic, I replied, "I love and trust you. You will take my heart with you when you leave. I look forward to hearing everything about your findings and ways of life in Vancouver through your letters."

January 25, 1969

It was a bittersweet moment as we walked toward Lufthansa's check-in counter. I heard the quiet humming of airport noise in a trance-like state and watched people come and go. I felt my soul transport into another world as the last piece of Juergen's luggage rolled out of sight on the conveyer belt.

Before he entered the departure door, we held each other tight, saying, "*Auf Wiedersehen.*" Until we meet again.

Then, all too soon, he was out of sight. In the distance, I heard our friends Joachim and his wife, Rhona, say, "This is goodbye for us, but you will see him again, Una."

Feeling emotionally drained, I walked back to the car in slow motion.

When I got home, Lance had left to spend the weekend with Vernon. After I soaked in a hot bath, Mumsie handed me a hot toddy. I awoke the following morning to the early morning sun rays streaming through the window with the feeling of a gaping hole in my stomach.

Empathy

I empathized with Mumsie. "I can't imagine how you must feel after Dad's death, being married for forty-four years. Why did you get married so young? You were barely sixteen, and Dad seventeen," I said.

With a faraway look, Mumsie began, "Times were different. In 1841, after my mother—your paternal grandmother—and her sisters migrated from St. Helena Island, my mother conceived me out of wedlock. She later married, and my stepfather adopted me. My mother bore my stepfather five children.

"My stepfather volunteered in the army during WWI to help support his family. The war lasted for four years, and at the same time, my mother suffered from ill health. Without proper healthcare, she could not work, leaving me to care for my siblings. At age sixteen, your dad and I married. My mother died two months before your sister, Maureen, was born. We continued to help rear my siblings long after my mother died."

I was astonished at my parents' fortitude at such a young age. Love and gratitude filled my heart.

"I salute you and Dad, Mumsie. I vaguely remember you telling us the story during my rebellious teen years. Please forgive me for the angst I caused."

"There's nothing to forgive. All your father and I hoped and prayed for were the safety and health of our children. Go to Canada and experience what your father and I never did. You have my full support. I will take care of Lance until you send for him," Mumsie confirmed.

"Thank you, Mumsie. I'll always love you," I sobbed.

We hugged each other and wiped away our tears.

"Now, I will make us a hot cup of tea, and we'll talk about happier times to come," Mumsie said, trying to lift my spirit.

Chapter Seventeen

Mumsie and I prepared lunch for my siblings, and their families set the tables for when they arrived after church with their potluck dishes. We set a separate table for Pearl (Fauzia) and her family's halal potluck for food allowed to be consumed under Islamic dietary guidelines.

Mumsie and I tried keeping the conversation light.

Curiosity

"I'm sure Juergen's parents will be glad to see him after his six-year stay in Johannesburg, and curious to know about his engagement to you," Mumsie said.

"Hmm," I replied, "It would be interesting to hear what his parents had to say about him marrying a divorcee with a child from another country and culture. When I first met Juergen, he told me he was glad to get away from the staunchness of German society and live an active life under blue skies and sunshine in Johannesburg. It's a shame he had to leave South Africa. Jeff's letter stated the winters are long, very cold, wet, and mostly cloudy in Vancouver."

"You'll have to invest in winter clothes," Mumsie reminded me.

After lunch, the men played darts and ring games. The curious felines gathered in Mumsie's bedroom, eagerly awaiting any news about Juergen. Lying on her bed, Mumsie was content surrounded by her daughters, daughter-in-law, Carol, and our cousin, Pamela.

Patsy hugged me, followed by the rest of the group. "We're sorry Juergen had to leave," they said.

"So am I. It will take a few days before I hear from Juergen through the mail. Let's not be sad. It's not over. Just the beginning. In the meantime, let's think happy thoughts," I said.

"We're excited for you. Wow! A new beginning in your life. We are all rooting for you, Sally," Maureen said.

"Thank you, that means a lot to me," I exclaimed.

"We heard the winters last for three months," said Patsy.

"You girls should go shopping at Woolworths Clothing for warm underwear for your sister before she leaves for Canada," Mumsie said.

"And maybe we can get some ideas for a wedding dress. In a magazine, I saw they wear lovely fur capes and hand muffs in those cold countries," Maureen, the romantic dreamer, said.

"I don't think we could afford a fur cape or hand muffs," I whispered.

"I remember how skinny you were when we fitted you for your first wedding dress. The dressmaker lined the waist with pockets stuffed with tissue paper to give it shape and added a hooped petticoat that made it extend out. Lord! I'm glad those days are over," my sister-in-law Carol exclaimed.

"They have high mountains covered in snow in Canada. I saw in a movie about how fast the snow slid down the mountain and buried the whole town, and they dug in the snow to save people. I would be afraid to live there," gasped Fauzia.

"You'll have to wear heavy boots and long skirts as they wear in the Western movies. They also have handsome cowboys," Patsy and Pamela squealed with delight.

"Seriously, what would you wear on your wedding day?" Maureen inquired.

"Well, let's not jinx it. Even though we don't know when or if the wedding will occur, we can have fun browsing for velvet material in my favourite colour, cornflower blue, and look for a wedding dress or skirt patterns. You are the dressmaker in the family, Fauzia. I would appreciate your input. Let's get together and think about a not-too-elaborate wedding dress. Will you sew it for me, Fauzia?"

"Of course, I will. You're my sister."

Everybody agreed it was a darn shame that they could not attend the wedding when it did take place.

Shifting uncomfortably in her chair, Maureen asked, "Ahem, do you think you will have more children, Sal?"

All Ears Perked Up

"Well, you know about the miscarriages I had when married to Vernon. And the scarring it left in my uterus. Even though Juergen and I have discussed this matter, I'm certain he would support me. I'm not sure I could go through all that trauma in a foreign country, though. Thank God I have Lance. Imagine if I were to conceive and have children here in Johannesburg, and my children had German and coloured features. One would have blonde hair and brown eyes, while the other had red hair or blue or green eyes. Lord! Wouldn't that send the Apartheid government into a quandary?"

Laughter erupted.

Maureen's husband David knocked on the bedroom door and said, "I hear a lot of laughter; you ladies must be having a good chitter-chatter. I'm sorry to break up the party, but it's getting late, and it's time to tuck the little ones in bed."

Before they left, "Let's go shopping next weekend. We'll search for a cowboy hat. I'm not sure about the cowboys," I said.

With a puzzled look, David raised his eyebrow and said, "Women!"

Hardly a week had passed when rumours circulated that Juergen had left me. Within the month, I received invitations to parties and weekend getaways from strangers with bogus addresses. Disgusted, I resealed the envelopes and returned them to the post office marked unknown. I sensed people staring at me, waiting for the other shoe to drop.

My family and I vowed Juergen had left me to throw rumour mongers off track. We made a pact not to speak to anybody about my pending immigration to Canada.

Advice

Aunt Kitty advised me to notify Juergen to forward all my mail to her home address in Rosebank, assuming my mail was tampered with in transit.

Ten days later, I received mail from Juergen via Aunt Kitty. The envelope contained photos of a joyous welcome home celebration with his parents and his sister. He wrote that he loved and missed me, and wished I could meet his family and join in the celebration. His parents had myriad questions about Lance and me and our pending marriage. They also wanted to know why he chose to start a new life in Canada and not Germany. He stated he chose Canada because it is a young country with the potential to grow.

Feeling optimistic at work on Monday morning, I answered an incoming call on the switchboard.

"Good morning, S. A. Bias Binding. Una speaking, how can I assist you?"

An Uncouth caller

In an unmannerly tone, the caller said, "Put this call through to my wife, Reena Van-Der-Hoff.

"Certainly, sir. One moment, please, while I transfer your call."

I transferred the call, but Reena was not at her desk. I then announced over the speaker, "Reena, you have a call waiting." Immediately after she had spoken with her husband, she approached me at the switchboard and aggressively said, "Una, my husband does not want you calling me Reena. He wants you to call me Mrs. Van-Der-Hoff."

A thousand past episodes spiralled through my mind. While Reena stood awaiting my rebuttal, I refused to be provoked, and I braced myself to continue answering incoming calls and jotting down several messages. Once the flashing lights on the switchboard subsided, I said to myself, "Hold your horses, Una."

Turning to Reena, I said, "I have a job to do. Please, leave and take your hostility with you. We will settle this during our lunch break."

Jerold, a salesman, watching the scene unfold, gave me the thumbs up.

During our lunch break, I called Reena and said, "If you expect me to address you by your last name, I look forward to the same from you." Reena glared at me and walked away. No love lost.

That evening, unannounced, Vernon fetched Lance to visit Gary, his newborn stepbrother, who was in the hospital.

With a smirk, Vernon sarcastically said, "So, I heard your boyfriend left you?"

Still fuming from the day's event at work, I would have spit nails if I wasn't dependent on Vernon signing the legal documents to enable Lance to leave the country.

After they left, I took a long walk around the neighbourhood to calm down. I missed my father and Juergen.

I screamed out loud, "If it's not one thing, it's another!"

As I sat crying on the swing in the park opposite our home, glaring lights from a police van shone the spotlight on me.

I jumped from the swing and ran back home. I met Vernon at the gate as he brought Lance back. He turned to see why I was running. As the police van passed us, Vernon looked at me questioningly, and neither of us said a word. I was thankful he was there at that moment.

I said, "Congratulations! Another son."

Vernon stared in space before he said, "Thank you."

"Why is your son in the hospital?" I asked.

"He was born with jaundice," Vernon replied.

"I hope he recovers soon," I responded.

"I'm the big brother," Lance bragged.

"Yes, big brother," I teased. "Let's hurry in and get ready for bed."

Mail from Vancouver

I received mail from Juergen. He noted that upon his arrival in Vancouver on February 20, it was damp and cold. He booked into the Grosvenor Hotel on Howe Street. The following day, Jeff and his parents, whom he had never met, fetched him, a total stranger, and welcomed him into their home in Lynn Valley. A week later, Juergen was employed at Schlage Lock Company in North Vancouver as a tool- and die-maker/design draftsman.

Now that he had his permanent residence status, he would follow through with obtaining the legal documents to sponsor me to enter Canada as his fiancée within the next six months. I was hoping Vernon would grant Lance's passport before then.

A month later, under the advice of a lawyer, it suggested Juergen avoid my sponsorship as documents were being disposed of by the Apartheid regime in Johannesburg. Instead, I should fly to Germany and stay with my future in-laws for a month. This would enable my sponsorship in Germany, where I must complete my medical examinations before obtaining my visa to Canada. Bile burned my throat at the thought of leaving Lance behind. I cussed Vernon for dragging his feet in approving Lance's passport.

This news riled me and set off a domino effect, reflecting on the stigmas of an unjust government and the events around me. I cussed the Apartheid regime for controlling my life and many others before me. They muted our voices, driving many to the brink of suicide. How many elders died of strokes due to human deprivation? How many Black men did not return home from the goldmines? How many were coerced to jump from twelve-storey buildings?

I compared the discriminatory punishment between the white police officer who raped a thirteen-year-old Black girl and got away with it; the coloured boy who raped a white girl and paid the penalty by being imprisoned. And the farmer who fathered a child with his Bantu maid. To avoid scandal, he abandoned the infant in the field. I shuddered at the fate of the innocent child. I thought about the poor Black children in Soweto, who were the worst off, which prompted me to write the poem:

Kumra

As the African sun dipped on the horizon.
You laughed with such glee as you listened to cricket's chirp.
While you knelt to pray, police officers kicked in the door of
your thatched-roof home.
The sole candle flickered and dimmed.

Flashlights glared in the darkness, voices shouted, and dogs barked.
You whimpered as the search continued.

You saw your father's shadow as he fled through the open window.
In the distance, you listened to the pounding of his footsteps.
Gunshots rang out!
Then silence.

Five-thirty, the cock crowed.
Soweto awoke as the first rays of sunlight streamed through the unhinged door.
As embers in the tin galley started to fade, you stared into space.
Wondering if the crickets would continue to chirp at dusk.
Would you ever hear your father's footsteps again?

Chapter Eighteen

Feelings of Anxiety

A lthough I was excited to leave and start a new life in Canada, I felt anxious, as though the doctor had told me I had six months to live. I wanted to enjoy everything possible before life as I knew it in South Africa ebbed away. The picture of Mumsie at sixteen tending to her brothers and sisters during WWI while her stepfather was away at war kept me company during my sleepless nights. I prayed I had inherited her fortitude.

Mumsie, in her infinite wisdom, calmed me down by saying, "You have nothing to lose. I will take care of Lance. Go to Canada. I have confidence Juergen will take good care of you. Maybe Vernon will realize it would be selfish to hold Lance back from obtaining a better life for himself. Lance would be able to make yearly visits to South Africa when he's older."

"I hoped Vernon would consider the option and not drag the legal battle on out of spite. It's always the children who suffer. Although it seemed like his resentment towards me had subsided now that he has a growing family," I commented.

"Who knows when we will see you again? We could never afford to visit you in Canada," Mumsie said, wiping away a tear.

I related the pain Mumsie felt to mine—her letting me go and me leaving my child behind. We hugged each other and sobbed.

"I promise I will come back and visit someday. Who knows, I might fetch Lance sooner," I added.

During the following months, our family and close, trusted friends spent every Saturday evening together, sharing meals, dancing to the old tunes of Elvis Presley, Engelbert Humperdinck, Percy Faith, and The Platters, and many other songs from long-playing records.

Shopping with My Sisters

At the beginning of autumn, temperatures hovered around 22 to 27°C, with up to twelve hours of daylight. Since the stores closed at 1 p.m., my sisters and I boarded a bus at 7 a.m. to afford the time to shop at the bargain layaway stores on 14th Street in Vrededorp. Customarily, if you were the first to enter a Jewish store, you were guaranteed a reasonable price on your first purchase. In contrast, you might be afforded the same courtesy if you were the last to enter a Muslim or Indian store before closing.

These stores had lots of shelving stacked to the ceilings with layaway purchases. Once, we witnessed an owner get knocked off a ladder by large parcels of layaways as they came tumbling down while he rummaged through paid-up parcels.

While searching amongst the bolts of velvet material during our shopping spree, Maureen found the exact colour of cornflower blue I had imagined for my wedding dress, including a couple of dress patterns. Still, before buying the material, we had to choose a design. We paid for our purchases and left the store excited to get home and peruse the designs.

We visited our grandfather's grave in Braamfontein, a cemetery within walking distance from 14th Street. Famished after the long day of hustling and bustling, we bought fish and chips wrapped in brown paper before entering the cemetery. We sat on the bench opposite the grave and ate lunch while enjoying the sunshine.

My Sponsorship

When we arrived home, I was ecstatic to receive mail from Juergen, in a large-padded envelope, containing photos of himself with the Laundy family, their home, and garden. He included many beautiful images of the surrounding area. He was glad to convey his progress in obtaining an interview with Canadian Immigration in September regarding my sponsorship. His parents were looking forward to meeting me when I arrived in Germany.

My family sat in the kitchen, eagerly awaiting the news. I passed around the photos. We were all surprised to see green grass and colourful flowers in the pictures, as we expected to see mounds of snow.

"I wonder how long it will take to get my visa after Juergen's interview with immigration?" I spoke.

"Well," said Patsy, "it sounds like the wedding will be soon. Let's look at the design patterns to see what suits best for velvet material."

Most of us fancied the off-the-shoulder, long-sleeved, knee-length pattern with the scalloped hem design.

That night, Lance crawled into bed next to me and rested his chin on his wrist, looking pensive. He asked, "How far is Canada? Is Juergen coming back, Mummy?"

I gathered him in my arms and said, "No, Juergen's not coming back. Canada is far, far away. Juergen will send us plane tickets when he has enough money. Would you like to fly in one of those big planes we saw at the airport?"

"Yes, I'm a big boy. I'm not afraid. Maybe my dad or Mumsie can give us some money?"

"We'll ask Mumsie if she can give us some money," I replied without suppressing Lance to keep our conversation a secret.

"OK. Mummy, I love you. Can I sleep in your bed tonight?"

"Yes, now say your prayers and let's sleep."

As I lay in the bed, I said, "Shit! Una, the cat's out of the bag. How are you going to get out of this one?"

The day before, Lance visited Vernon. I was in turmoil about how I would respond if Lance innocently asked Vernon about money for our plane tickets.

Weary when Vernon fetched Lance, I blurted out, "When do you think we will complete all the legal papers for Lance's passport? I'm considering leaving for Australia or Canada to start a new life for Lance and myself."

Taken aback, there was an awkward moment between us before Vernon muttered in response, "We'll see about that."

Lance darted out of the house and toward us. As he hugged me, he said, "See you on Sunday, Mummy."

I wanted to avoid an argument in Lance's presence. "Think about it. Wouldn't you wish all your children to have a better life?" I questioned.

He glared at me, took Lance's hand, and walked away.

After visiting Vernon, I asked Lance, "Why do you look sad?"

"My dad was fighting again. Can I stay home next time and play with Charles and Brian, Mummy?" he begged.

"Of course, you can!" I responded.

A Mother's Protection

Discouraged from hearing the disappointment in Lance's voice, I conjured up the worst scenario: maybe Vernon and his wife were arguing because she felt obligated to Lance's visits. Perhaps he spends too much time with Lance during his visits. There could be myriad reasons.

Like a tigress wanting to protect her cub, fierceness rose inside me. First thing on Monday, I phoned my lawyer to set up an appointment regarding visitation and other legal matters. Feeling angst while waiting in the foyer at the lawyer's office, I stared at a picture on the wall of a boy surfing. I closed my eyes and envisioned myself riding the waves, which had a calming effect on me.

I walked into the lawyer's office, bound and determined to state my case. I would not tolerate having Lance subjected to any aggression between Vernon and his wife, nor any passive-aggressive behaviour toward Lance by any other influence.

Should the matter reoccur, I would not hesitate to schedule an intake interview, whereby each parent and a monitor would meet to discuss the case.

I inquired about the progress of Lance's passport and the ramifications of relocating and the process of me appointing Mumsie as Lance's custodian if I were to be out of the country. I implied that if I was granted sole custody, I would forego maintenance support and award Vernon yearly visitation rights, sharing travelling costs. I thanked the lawyer and left it in his hands until further notice. I felt as if my ship weighed anchor, and I was headed to an unknown destination. I was yet to feel buoyant, knowing there was no reward without risk.

As my birthday approached, I thought of when I married Vernon at age twenty-one. I would have never envisioned myself fighting for sole custody of our son. I informed Vernon that Lance would be away the weekend of his upcoming visitation. We agreed for him to have Lance the following weekend. After that, visitation continued without incident.

In the middle of April, Vernon and I went to mediation to discuss sole custody in the child's best interest, highlighting the positive/negative aspects. Vernon and I could not agree to schedule a follow-up date through our lawyers.

At the end of June, Juergen's letter read:

Una, my love, I'm overwhelmed with emotion and antici-pation to let you know that my interview with Canadian Immigration has unexpectedly sped. On June 20, I handed in all my legal documents and other required records. I proved that I could support a family. I explicitly said you would enter Canada from Germany and requested you enter Canada before year's end so we could be married before the New Year.

It required that I write a handwritten letter to confirm my intention. Without hesitation, I wrote a signed letter of my purpose to marry you within the following six months upon your arrival in Canada, and I handed it to him. This interviewing officer cautioned me that before my sponsorship for you becomes legal, it would depend on you passing all required medical tests in Germany to get a visa to enter Canada.

I'm sure that after reading the above, you're as over-whelmed as I am. I hope the sudden speed of change and uncertainties in your life will not deter our dreams and love for each other. I await your reply.

Yours,

Juergen

A Welcome Surprise

In July, I had a surprise visit by my ex-mother-in-law, whom I had no qualms with and had no contact with for over five years. I invited her in for tea. She returned the wedding album I left behind.

"I thought Lance would appreciate this one day," she said.

"Thank you! I'm sure he will," I agreed.

During her visit, she flipped through the album and noted the likeness of Lance to his father. She avoided eye contact with me. "You and Vernon were so happy on your wedding day."

"And young and naïve," I replied.

An air of melancholy surrounded her when I alluded to my intention of obtaining sole custody of Lance. Without animosity between us, we hugged each other before she left.

I experienced a whirlwind of emotions. Fauzia finished sewing my wedding dress. There were many *ooh-aahs* as I modelled, twirled, and curtsied, thanking Fauzia for a well-done job. Mumsie wiped away a tear.

Melancholy

I felt time slipping away, and I held onto Lance tighter each day, reminding him that as sure as day follows the night, I would send for him. I realized getting sole custody was going to be expensive and time-consuming. My lawyer would have to prepare a detailed custody plan that evaluated the facilities and resources in the new location, including the cost of living, schools, and cultural environment in the child's best interest.

The distant echoing sound of Black mineworkers singing in tandem as they worked, despite the hardships they endured, the wandering remnants of the simple home in Vrededorp and the memories of laughter and tears that my family and I shared ran through my mind. It will always be a remembrance of where my life began.

Chapter Nineteen

M y departure loomed. As September's spring heat sizzled to 32ºC, apple and peach trees were laden with fruit. Jacaranda tree blossoms coated the roads in a purple carpet. The mood in our home hovered between anticipation, excitement, sadness, and weepy.

I amused my family by practicing my German guttural sounds. Juergen's parents did not speak English. I was terrified at the thought of communicating with them. While I awaited my visa in Germany, would they accept me into their family? I would always have a home to return to, whatever happened.

I amiably approached Vernon in desperation, saying, "You have a growing family now. Why deprive me of mine?"

"We'll talk about it when you return," he said.

As a departure gift, I received a lovely blue hard-sided Samsonite luggage set from my colleagues at S. A. Bias Binding.

All Too Soon

And so, the time came all too soon. I booked a Lufthansa flight to Germany at the end of October 1969. My pending departure left me in a state of suspended animation.

On my departure, Leon, my uncle, drove us to the airport. Lance tugged at my jacket and asked, "When will you send me a ticket, Mummy?"

I choked up and looked over at Mumsie as tears welled up in my eyes. Putting up a brave front, I swallowed hard and said, "Remember, I promised I would send for you as soon as I get a job and get some money. Listen to Mumsie and your dad. Do all your homework, and don't forget to say your prayers, OK. I will write you letters and send lots of photos."

We found a quiet spot and said a departing prayer. We were restraining ourselves, not crying in Lance's presence. Before departing, with a broken heart, I said, "Keep the faith, and remember that I love you." I gave Lance a big hug and reminded him of my promise.

I sat at the window next to the wing. As the airplane slowly took off from the runway, I felt numb as the aircraft ascended over the bright lights of the city of gold. As I looked down from my window seat, the plane banked as the sun slowly set on the horizon like a giant ball of fire.

It emphasized the actual gold mine dumps, where a trusted family friend took my innocence twenty-two years before. I had an out-of-body experience as I relived the scene. The sound of his voice and warning, "Don't you dare tell anybody." It reverberated in my senses above the drone of the aircraft. I realized I could never cancel my past. With pent-up emotions, I sobbed for my child and family. Then, it dawned on me that the whole casting of my life lay wide open.

International Flight

I was mentally and emotionally exhausted during my first international flight. The airplane white noise lulled me to sleep during the ten-hour flight from Johannesburg to Frankfurt, when the plane touched down on the tarmac. It startled me when the passengers clapped their hands to appreciate a safe landing. Disembarking from the plane in Frankfurt, it was snowing, as it was the middle of November, with a freezing temperature of -4ºC, compared to the 25-plus-degree temperature when I left Johannesburg. I was stunned at the vastness of the airport: the sight of all the shuttle buses lined up to transport passengers to their terminal flight connections, people dressed in warm coats, jackets, boots, and some carrying ski equipment. I looked around for signs in English.

I said to myself, "Du bist jetzt in Deutschland." *You are in Germany now.* I strained my ears to the German phonic sounds, boarded a shuttle bus, and found the terminal to my inland flight to Hamburg, where Juergen's parents and his younger sister Helga awaited my arrival. "How should I address his parents?" I thought. "Frau Kohfeldt und Herr Kohfeldt?"

My heart pounded as I entered through the arrival gate. I anxiously scanned the crowd for faces resembling those in a familiar photograph. It did not take long.

Helga ran up to greet me, "Hallo, Una," she excitedly exclaimed.

"Hello, Helga," I replied.

That would be the last English word I voiced for the following month.

Juergen's mother, a beautiful, blue-eyed, blonde-haired, middle-aged woman, was dressed stylishly, wearing a brown fedora with a green feather and a fur coat. Dressed in a black polo-neck sweater was Juergen's stepfather. In unison, they said, "Willkommen in Deutschland." *Welcome to Germany.*

"Guten abend, Frau Kohfeldt und Herr Kohfeldt. Danke schön," I replied.

We arrived at his parent's two-bedroom apartment. Helga and I carried my luggage up four flights of tiled stairs, as there were no elevators. After I had a hot shower and changed clothes, we celebrated my arrival.

Juergen's mother said, "Please, address us as Muti und Vati." *Mother and Father.*

It took a while before I wrapped "Muti und Vati" around my tongue.

There were many questions about Lance, my family, and how I met Juergen. It took a considerable amount of brain energy to convert and answer all the questions accurately in the German language. It left me exhausted.

Shopping With My Future Mother-In-Law

Upon awakening the following morning, I witnessed ice flowers on the windowpanes for the first time. After breakfast, before Juergen's mother and I went shopping for winter boots and warm undergarments, I sent Mumsie a telegram to let her know I had arrived safely and missed them.

On our way home, we dropped in at the local bakery where Juergen's mother bought pastries, and we waited while the owner ground freshly roasted coffee beans and put them in a brown paper bag. It smelled delicious.

The following weeks were hectic. I had doctor's appointments, blood tests, X-rays, and interviews in preparation for my Canadian visa. After weeks of prodding and questioning, I longed to converse in English. I phoned Mumsie to update her on meeting Juergen's family and their kindness in accepting me. I spoke with Lance and reassured him of my promise and that I loved and missed him.

The German eating habits were different. They ate a lot of cold cut meats, cheese, and pumpernickel bread, along with dark, heavy, and slightly sweet rye bread and coffee for breakfast. Lunch was yummy lentil soup loaded with ham and tiny potatoes. Dinner included schnitzel and red cabbage/pork and sauerkraut. After a heavy meal, we had a tablespoon of Jagermeister, a cold herbal essence comprising of fifty-six selected botanical herbs in thirty-five percent alcohol matured in oak. I feared I might put on weight and not fit my wedding dress. Each evening, we watched German television, giving me a reprieve from conversing—which I'm sure worked both ways.

Before retiring for the night, I wrote a letter to Mumsie.

Dear Mumsie,

I hope you are all well and that Lance is coping with me leaving without him.

After my heartbreaking departure, as the plane flew over the city's bright lights, memories flooded my mind. I thanked God for giving me you. Without you, I would not be who I am. You and Dad gave us love, strength, and safety, and instilled faith and hope in our lives.

Thank you for always being there for all of us. Most of all, thank you for taking care of Lance and allowing me to find a better life for Lance and myself.

I arrived in Frankfurt, Germany, with the temperature at -4. I was stunned at the vastness of the airport and all the shuttle busses lined up to transport passengers to various terminals. All bundled up in warm jackets, they were hustling and bustling, with some carrying ski equipment.

After the second leg of my journey, I continued to Hamburg on an inland flight. Juergen's parents and his sister Helga were amicable in welcoming me, which was a great relief. Since then, everybody's been helpful.

The processing of my visa continues. There are many changes to adapt to; it gets dark early and the sun rises late. Then there is the different language. Thank God for the Berlitz School of Language. But I'm managing, so don't fret. People are very accommodating. His mother gifted me a lovely pair of fur-lined leather boots with good traction, preventing me from slipping on the icy roads and the snow. It takes getting used to the frigid cold.

Oh! How I miss soaking in a hot tub. Most apartments have showers; tap water is expensive and used sparingly. It's in and out when taking a shower. The bed coverings are comforters that are two layers of regular thin outer fabric filled with goose-down (feathers) instead of blankets. It surprised me how light it was, yet it kept me comfortably warm. It's custom to remove your shoes upon entering the apartment. Tell my sisters I'm getting accustomed to wearing boots.

Please give Lance a big kiss and hug him tight for me. I'll send photos next time, and arrange another phone call soon. I miss all of you so very much. You are always in my prayers.

Lots of kisses for Lance. Xxxxxxxx.

Tons of love,

Sally.

Hamburg/Germany

There were festive gatherings and introductions to other relatives and friends in the following weeks, including German Christmas delicacies of rabbit, goose, and stollen—a fruit bread of nuts, spices, and dried candied fruit containing marzipan (ground almonds.) I was questionable about the steak tartare, an open-faced sandwich with raw ground beef, onions, capers, and Worcestershire sauce.

I missed the closeness, laughter, and hugs my family and I shared with friends when greeting. I tried not to be intimidated when conversing in German amidst a group of heavy smokers. I observed body language and controlled smiles. I listened and remained humble. I answered questions as best as possible, according to my newly learned knowledge of the German language.

A guest asked, "What do you think about Apartheid?"

I replied, "I do not have to think about it. I lived it."

He glared at me and shifted in his chair.

Before he could answer, Juergen's stepfather came to the rescue and announced, "It's getting late. We have a busy morning ahead. The conversation can continue the next time we meet."

I felt a weight lift off my shoulders as my German waned.

It excited me to receive a call from Juergen. He hoped the embassy would approve my visa soon, and looked forward to my arrival. He mentioned that he was looking for an apartment to rent, and we would furnish it together when I arrived.

The Laundy family was looking forward to meeting me, and we had an open dinner invitation pending. His employment satisfied him, and we agreed we would chomp at the bit to obtain Lance's passport once I settled in.

Christmas was fast approaching, and the Canadian Embassy would be shut down for the holiday season. I felt sad at the thought that I might not be leaving Germany until the new year. Two weeks later, upon receiving my Canadian visa, I was overjoyed and expressed to Juergen's family that I wished to leave Germany before Christmas. They showed disappointment in not having the time to get to know me.

December 1969 – My Journey Resumes

Giddy with excitement, I said, "Auf Wiedersehen" to Juergen's family.

As my journey continued, I was astounded to learn about the different Canadian time zones. I shut my eyes, and my head was literally in the clouds, contemplating my future challenges. My next stop was Montréal, Canada. Then onward to my new home in North Vancouver, British Columbia.

In defiance of the Immorality Act, seeking a haven, mother and child separate. One in South Africa, the other in Canada. On challenging journeys, we find out who we are.